Living Dharma

The Teachings of Sri Dharma Pravartaka Acharya

Editor
Tulasi Devi Mandaleshvari

www.dharmacentral.com

Other Books by
Sri Dharma Pravartaka Acharya

Sanatana Dharma: The Eternal Natural Way

The Sanatana Dharma Study Guide

Consciousness Wars

My Religion is Sanatana Dharma

The Vedic Way of Knowing God

Radical Universalism: Are All Religions are the Same?

The Art of Wisdom: Affirmations for Boundless Living

The Shakti Principle: Encountering the Feminine Power of God

Taking Refuge in Dharma: The Initiation Guidebook

Living Dharma: The Teachings of Sri Dharma Pravartaka Acharya

The Vedic Encyclopedia

Vedanta: The Culmination of Wisdom

The Dharma Dialogues

The Dharma of Wellbeing

The Dharma of Leadership

Eine Einführung in den Vedanta: Ausgewählte Vorträge von Sri Dharma Pravartaka Acharya

Mantra Meditations (CD)

These works can be purchased at:

Dharmacentral.com

Sri Dharma Pravartaka Acharya
Founder-President
International Sanatana Dharma Society

Dedication

This work is dedicated to
Sri Srimad
A.C. Bhaktivedanta Swami Prabhupada

Introduction

Sanatana Dharma is the Eternal Natural Way. It is the most ancient continuously practiced religious tradition on Earth, and at one time in history it served as the spiritual foundation of every healthy society and civilization on earth. It is known today in its more popular name of "Yoga spirituality". Sanatana Dharma is a living tradition that has stood the test of time, and that is as relevant today for sincere spiritual practitioners as it was in the most ancient of times. More, it is a spiritual tradition that can only be fully appreciated and experienced if it is lived as a dedicated lifestyle of daily practice under the guidance of an authentic and highly qualified spiritual master (*guru*).

The following collection of short wisdom teachings have been revealed by just such a qualified teacher, Sri Dharma Pravartaka Acharya, over a span of several years in his teaching career. In these powerful and enlightening teachings, we gain a precious and rare glimpse of the very essence of Dharma, as well as practical guidance for how we can practice Dharma and Yoga spirituality in an authentic, meaningful and effective way. These wisdom sayings come directly from the pen of one of the world's foremost living Dharma Masters, leaders and authors. So, the information that they contain are a spiritual treasure for us.

The contents of *Living Dharma: The Teachings of Sri Dharma Pravartaka Acharya* cover a wide range of topics, both philosophical and practical. This great diversity of topics is very much by design, since there is no aspect of the human experience that Dharma does not touch upon directly and conclusively. Thus, while each one of these short wisdom sayings will provide a deeply spiritual vision to the reader, some of them also comment upon such seemingly "secular" aspects of human thought as psychology, politics, economics, social science, culture, aesthetics and health. The only way to truly incorporate the teachings of Sanatana Dharma into your life is to practice Dharma in every single aspect of your life, without exception. This is exactly what *Living Dharma* was created to help you do.

It is precisely with this integrative vision of Dharma in mind that Sri Acharyaji insisted that the various aphorisms in this work not be artificially grouped together by specific topics. Rather, the aphorisms perfectly convey the underlying spiritual concern uniting all the various topics and fields of human endeavor. In this work, your awareness will flow naturally from one field to another, one science to another, one academic discipline to another, one dimension of reality to another. The underlying thread that unites all the varying thought in this book is Dharma spirituality. Whether commenting upon spirituality, politics, philosophy, economics, history or Yoga, each aphorism boldly reveals the deepest spiritual essence lying within all fields of human concern, waiting to be discovered by the reader.

All of these brief wisdom teachings are in themselves powerfully effective meditation sessions, and in order to derive the greatest benefit from them, they should be treated as such. Take your time in reading and deeply contemplating each of these valuable spiritual jewels. Read them repeatedly, and with an open and receptive mind. Allow your inner being to absorb their power and their truth. They have much more to reveal to you than you may at first detect on a mere surface level reading. Allow Sri Acharyaji's words of wisdom to accompany you in your everyday travels and to speak to the depths of your soul. Live Dharma spirituality...and allow Dharma to live in you.

Though any sincere reader will derive benefit from this work, this book is especially meant for the serious spiritual seeker. If you can fully understand and apply its sacred teachings to your life, with humility, sincerity, openness and enthusiasm, your life will be radically transformed for the better.

For more in-depth information on the history, philosophy and practice of Dharma spirituality, please read Sri Dharma Pravartaka Acharya's *magnum opus* work *Sanatana Dharma: The Eternal Natural Way.*

Tulasi Devi Mandaleshvari
Editorial Manager and Layout Designer
General Manager
International Sanatana Dharma Society
November, 2011
Omaha, NE, USA

Dharmacentral.com

Introduction to 2017 Printing

It has been just a little over six years since the first printing of *Living Dharma*. In this brief period of time, many thousands of readers have lauded the life-changing benefits they have experienced from this remarkable book, as well as the brilliance of its author. We are happy to now introduce the second, expanded and enhanced, printing of this important work by Sri Dharma Pravartaka Acharya. In addition to the inclusion of hundreds of new aphorisms, this new edition now has a detailed index for greater ease of use, research and reference. We offer special thanks Ms. Kalpana Mathema for her wonderful service in creating the new index.

Tulasi Devi Mandaleshvari
Editorial Manager and Layout Designer
General Manager
International Sanatana Dharma Society
February, 2017
Omaha, NE, USA

www.dharmacentral.com

Preface By
Sri Dharma Pravartaka Acharya

While visiting my *diksha* (initiation) *guru's* beautiful *ashram* in rural India in 1986, my *guru*, B.R. Sridhara Swami Maharaja, gave me the formidable task to go back to America and to, myself, serve in the role of a *guru*. As he looked into my eyes, sitting no more than three or four feet away from me, he stated emphatically to me, "Now you must go back to America and teach them what you have learned. You must now be a *guru* in America and teach them about Krishna. That is your duty." It was only with a tremendous amount of initial trepidation on my part, and upon the force of my *guru's* orders, that I began attempting to fulfill his order soon after this pure, liberated being left our world.

I have been officially serving in the role of an Acharya, a Vedic teacher, since 1988. In all of these years, I have had the opportunity to meet many thousands of sincere spiritual seekers who have allowed me to serve my own *guru* through my very imperfect attempts to convey to them the truth of Vedic spirituality.

It has only been by the grace of my *gurus* that I have been personally able to understand and convey the teachings of Sanatana Dharma in a pure and authentic way. I offer my deepest respects to my revered *gurus*: Sri Devarshi Narada Muni, Sri Natha Muni, Sri Yatiraja Acharya, Srila Prabhupada and B.R. Sridhara Swami. I ask that their blessings be upon me, upon all of my sincere students, and upon the International Sanatana Dharma Society always.

I am exceedingly grateful to my very faithful student, Mandaleshvari Tulasi Devi, for collecting these short teaching statements that were uttered by me over the years in formal talks that I delivered, as well as in conversations and communications that I had with others over the many years that I have been teaching. That she would put in such an amazing amount of work recording, arranging, editing and formatting this book of my sayings has left me humbled by her dedication to my teachings, and to the teachings of Sanatana Dharma. May she be remembered and honored forever by all beings for her service to Dharma.

It is my hope that the readers will derive great spiritual benefit from contemplating the words in this wonderfully constructed volume, and that their understanding and experience of Vedic spirituality will significantly deepen as a result.

Aum Shanti,
Dharma Pravartaka Acharya
February, 2017

Acknowledgements

Special thanks to Srimati Kalpana Mathema for her wonderful help. Thank you, also, to Dr. David Frawley, Sri Yogini Shambhavi Chopra, Sri Swami Dayananda Saraswati, Dharmaraja, Arjuna, Shakti Devi, Vishnuchitta, Vaidya Savitri Devi, Ramanuja, and Premananda.

1

Sanatana Dharma represents the loving grace of God manifest in the material world in the form of natural law. Natural law is how we experience God's grace within the material world. It is, therefore, by following God's natural law with dedication that we open ourselves up to the abundance of His divine grace. And it is by God's grace that we have the wisdom to fully know and honor His natural law. Dharma is God's rescue rope for all suffering beings, and the medium through which we can reconnect with Him. Dharma is God's gift to all creation. There is no greater means for knowing Truth in this world.

2

In order to experience the pure *atman* (soul), and to have a taste of the ecstatic bliss of self-realization and God-consciousness, the Vedic scriptures advise us to pursue spiritual life in a systematic and disciplined way. We accomplish this by meditating daily on the divine names of God (Aum Namo Narayanaya), by the spiritual practice of Yoga, by studying God's sacred instructions, such as the *Bhagavad Gita* and the *Srimad Bhagavatam*, and by cultivating such qualities as sincerity, humility, devotion, and compassion in our hearts. We must do this all under the expert guidance of a qualified *guru*. This is the essence of the Vedic way.

3

The *Bhagavad Gita* is the most advanced spiritual teaching available to humanity in our present age, known as the Kali Yuga. The *Bhagavad Gita* is the very heart of the entire Vedic literature. The heart of the *Bhagavad Gita*, in turn, is the spiritual path of Yoga. The very heart of Yoga is the practice of meditation. The heart of meditation is *bhakti*, or devotional consciousness toward Bhagavan Sri Krishna, who is the very center of the entire *Gita*. Thus, the actual heart of the *Bhagavad Gita* is Sri Krishna Himself.

4

Yoga spirituality was never intended to be a business. It is not a moneymaking venture. There is nothing either new, or 'new age', about Yoga. Yoga is an applied philosophy designed to lead its practitioner to a state of transcendental consciousness. The sole purpose of the spiritual and philosophical tradition of Yoga is to live a life of authenticity, a life in which we manifest the transcendent truth of our own eternal self as a mirror of God's love toward all beings. If we can live without greed, without envy, without lust, without selfishness, and without excuses, only then will we know the true purpose of Yoga.

5

The very heart of Sanatana Dharma is the practice of the path of Yoga. The heart of the path of Yoga is, in turn, meditation. It is only if we are steeped in a serious, deep and regular meditation practice that we can claim to be truly practicing Sanatana Dharma and Yoga spirituality in any meaningful way.

6

The true spiritual path does not originate from petty subjective opinions or prejudices, but from the eternal Absolute Reality. The most destructive mistake that one can make spiritually is to try to mix and match the teachings of different religious paths just to suit one's own self-calculating ends. Rather, the only way to make meaningful spiritual progress is to eventually surrender to one specific path, and to remain with that path faithfully until the goal is achieved. Steadiness, patience, fidelity and focus are the signs of mature spiritual practice. It is only with such focused dedication to one path that you will know God.

7

Aum Tat Sat. The two keys to success in Yoga, in meditation, and in spiritual life in general are consistent practice (*abhyasa*) and detachment (*vairagya*). There is no spiritual advancement or enlightenment without having a dedicated practice that we observe with faithfulness each and every day. There is no such thing as instant enlightenment. However, spiritual practice must also be performed without impatience, fear or anxiety. This is the nature of practice in detachment. If we follow this prescription of detached practice, coupled with the deep dedication of *bhakti* (devotional consciousness), we will know spiritual success. Aum Shanti.

8

Humility is one of the most important qualities that a true *yogi* will possess. Humility is the natural result of the gradual abandonment of ego, and the corresponding awaking of the true self. The result is a realistic assessment of who and what we are in relation to others. No one can be said to have achieved a deep level of spiritual realization if they do not display sincere humility in their lives. To know God is to know that you are God's servant. To know that you are God's servant is to know that you are the servant of all living beings.

9

Aum Namo Bhagavate Vasudevaya. The center of reality is also the ultimate source of all love, all good, and all sweetness. Bhagavan (God) alone is that center. That center lies temporarily hidden within your very own heart (*hridaya*). Access that spiritual center by meditating upon the sacred names of Bhagavan Sri Krishna. Know that center and you will know all. Aum Sri Krishnaya Namaha.

10

Dharma is nothing less that the ever-flowing descent of God's grace and love as that grace becomes concretized in the material world in the form of natural law and justice. Natural law is predicated upon God's grace. Dharma is the manifestation of God's infinite love. Therefore, it is in living a life of Dharma that we come to know God.

11

Aum Hari Aum. Our present materialistic culture has convinced too many of us that the entire world exists merely to serve our own personal needs. It does not. Rather, we ourselves exist for the sole purpose of serving God and serving our fellow living beings with compassion, patience and love. It is in following such a life of selfless dedication to those who lay outside of ourselves that we come to know our true selves. Aum Tat Sat.

12

In seeking either healing, or happiness, or positive social-political change, or Truth, or self-realization, we must always seek the root, and not merely the leaves. The root of the tree of existence is God. He is the source of all reality. Access to that root of all things is found in the wisdom of the Vedic scriptures. Plunge yourself into that ocean of sweet nectar known as the Vedic scriptures to know that root source of all. Every other concern that preoccupies the mind of man is merely peripheral to that root of all existence.

13

Aum Hari Aum. It is by one-pointed, devotional meditation upon the Divine that we purify our minds, open our hearts to His grace, experience our imprisoning egos melt away, and awaken freely to our natural constitutional state as eternal loving servants of the Absolute. This is the path of Bhakti Yoga, the king of all Yogas. It is through the path of Bhakti Yoga that we can achieve the highest of all spiritual aims. Aum Tat Sat.

14

The vast majority of present-day politicians and governments throughout the globe have now become the corrupt enemies of liberty, and of the very people they falsely claim to represent. Such corrupt politicians and governments are serving the malevolent purposes of hidden interests, and not those of the people. We must change this current course of corruption that our governments are steeped in. It is the sages and seers who are the true leaders of society, and not corrupt politicians. The time has now come for *sadhus* (sages) and virtuous *yogis* to guide the ship of state. Such Dharmic governance would ensure the happiness and prosperity of all. May wise and compassionate *yogis* soon replace every corrupt politician upon the Earth. Evam bhavatu. May it be so.

15

Aum Hari Aum. People are living in a media constructed version of reality, and not in reality itself. Reject the shackles of this artificially imposed reality. Reject the consciousness warping propaganda of the controlled media. Embrace instead the unalterable truth of your own eternal consciousness and of God's unlimited love. Reality is not the perverse nightmare that the media falsely portrays. Reality is sweet. Aum Tat Sat.

16

Bhakti, or single-minded devotional meditation upon Bhagavan (God), has always been, by its very inherent nature, the most powerful and dynamic social force on earth. *Bhakti* is an unparalleled motivating force that has induced revolutionary and meaningful change throughout world history. It has inspired the greatest poetry, the profoundest philosophy, the most breathtaking art, and the greatest personal sacrifices from its devotees. It will also serve as the driving spiritual force that will revive and strengthen Dharma well into the 21st Century. The only meaningful revolution is a revolution based on spiritual love.

17

Many mistakenly see Yoga as merely a system of physical training that also just *happens* to have a spiritual component to it as an afterthought. In actuality, Yoga is primarily a purely spiritual path, the sole goal of which is union ("*yoga*") with the Divine. The fact that Yoga also has a physical component to it is by design. The physical aspects (*asanas*) of Yoga exist in order to help the *yogi* to have wonderful health, and to develop the ability to sit for long periods of time in a proper meditation posture. It is only when we have fully embraced the spiritual purpose of Yoga, in both wisdom and practice, that we can claim to be *yogis* in the true sense of the term.

18

Authentic spirituality is never pursued for self-centered interests. True spirituality is more than merely focusing on our own personal psychological healing, gaining supposed mystical powers, yearning for control over our environment and over others, or trying to save ourselves alone. True spirituality also means having a sense of compassionate giving toward all living beings. To help others to embrace Truth and to improve themselves in every way is the highest welfare work that one can perform.

19

Satsangha means association with the good, the eternal, and the real. It is by proximity with goodness that we become good. By being close to the *guru*, to God, and to our fellow practitioners, we become like them and are positively transformed. Always seek *satsangha* at every opportunity. Always seek the association only of the good.

20

Aum Hari Aum. As *atman* (soul), we have our own individual existence situated in attributive, devotional relationship with Brahman (God). We have existence in order to know, to love, and to serve God. Let us make the most of our existence by pursuing spiritual liberation, and reestablishing ourselves in our natural constitutional position as servants of the Divine.

21

Bhakti (devotional consciousness) is meditation in its fullest and deepest manifestation. It is through the process of *bhakti* that the veil of illusion is lifted from our eyes; and it is in the devotional state of *bhakti* consciousness that we know God most intimately. *Bhakti* represents the deepest communion between God and human. It is, thus, not merely a path to achieve liberation. It is the very goal of the path. Aum tad vishno paramam padam.

22

Aum. The ultimate goal of Sanatana Dharma is to know, to love, and to serve Bhagavan, or God. It is in loving absorption (*samadhi*) in the Absolute that we fulfill our deepest purpose, and know our greatest joy. Every other endeavor that we are capable of - either material or spiritual - is secondary to this one ultimate goal. Aum.

23

One of the most important spiritual qualities that the *yogi* needs to develop within himself if he is to know success on the spiritual path is known as *sthiti-sthapaka*, or a deep sense of resilience. The spiritual path of Yoga is long. It is difficult. It is not a path that is meant for everyone, but only for the determined few. But with resilience, we can achieve success on this path. Always be resilient in your practice of Yoga spirituality, and you will know God.

24

While it would be foolish to deny the actual existence of empirical reality, it is even more foolish to claim that empirical reality is the foremost or only reality. Our perceptions of the empirical reality that we experience around us each day are real only in a secondary, derivative sense. Rather, what we experience through our material senses – while definitely real on the material level – is only a pale shadow of the spiritual Reality that is our home and that is the basis of our true being. The objects, situations, and causality of this sensory realm are all temporary. But the nature of the highest, spiritual Reality is eternal. It is a Reality that transcends the element of time, and that finds its center situated in the Absolute. Know and experience that foundational spiritual Reality first, and everything about this secondary material reality will consequently be revealed to you. Know God, and you know all.

25

Truth is not merely the opposite of falsehood, nor is it an intellectual exercise, nor merely a subjective opinion, nor just a cool faddish pursuit to make us seem more intelligent in the eyes of others. Truth is the very manifestation of God. God is Truth. Truth is the only thing that is truly real, and that truly matters. Truth is thus meant to be not only thought, but is meant to be lived. Live a life of Truth if you wish to know God.

26

Aum. It is in expressing compassion toward those around us who are suffering that we most fully express the beauty of our own true, spiritual self. To give is to express beauty. For this reason, the enlightened sage is the most beautiful person of all, because they give the greatest gift of all - enlightenment. Aum.

27

True spirituality is not about the acquisition of subtle mystic powers, psychic tricks, or dominion over others. Such worthless material pursuits in the name of spirituality are merely a form of Spiritual Egotism. These are not a measure of one's personal spiritual attainment. Rather, the true degree of personal spiritual advancement is measured by how much one has transcended illusory ego and the need to dominate others in order to satisfy that illusory ego. True spirituality is about having the courage, the determination, and the intelligence to surrender oneself wholly at the lotus-like feet of the Divine. It is in relinquishing the illusory ego in surrender to Sriman Narayana that we achieve true and meaningful spiritual liberation.

28

The soul (*atman*) is not merely an aspect, nor even merely a significant component, of the person, but actually is the person. It is not merely the case that you have a soul. You are soul. You are *atman.* Live each day knowing that you are soul, and you will know peace and joy in your life.

29

The key to meeting your life's daily challenges is to always be aware that you are an eternal spark of God. You are spirit. You are eternal, perfect and full of joy.

30

Your life is filled with a profound personal meaning deeper than you may presently fully know. You were meant from the very moment of your own birth to know intimately the happiness, contentment, peace, and bliss that naturally radiate from your true self. You are a child born of overflowing spiritual nectar, born of God's love, and who is destined to taste the sweet bliss of spirit yet again.

31

We are infinitely more than merely our bodies, our race, our ethnicity, or our religion. Our true self lies beyond the body, emotions, mind, intellect, and ego. We are eternal spirit, *atman*. We are free, blissful, and a reflection of God.

32

Aum. The Sadguru, the true *guru*, has the ability to impart Truth unto us, for he has himself bathed his being in wisdom. The true *guru* can show us how to love, for he personifies compassion toward all. The true *guru* has the power to liberate us, for he has traveled to the other shore, and tasted deeply of the nectar of freedom. Aum Sri Gurubhyo Namaha.

33

The most ancient and foundational of all *mantras* is the *mantra* Aum. First revealed as far back as the *Rig Veda* (circa 3,800 BCE), the *mantra* Aum is found in every known scripture of the Sanatana Dharma tradition. Aum is both a name of God, as well as the sound representation of God's omni-presence in reality. It is Aum that upholds all of reality, and that provides existence itself for all things.

34

Through Yoga, daily meditation, a healthy lifestyle, being an ethical person, and expressing loving compassion toward all, choose to make this present life a vehicle for spiritual renewal and rejoicing. These are the essential practices of Sanatana Dharma. Take full advantage of the precious gift of having a human form of life by incorporating these practices into your daily routine. Aum Tat Sat.

35

Aum. Let your own sincerity, humility, openness to the teachings of the Sadguru, and deep yearning to serve God be the vehicle that carries you swiftly to truth. This is what constitutes the vehicle of Dharma. Aum.

36

Wisdom and true knowledge are the most powerful possessions that you can acquire. It is in listening with patience and deep humility that you gain wisdom and true knowledge. Fools are always speaking, being in love with the sound of their own voice. But the wise know the discipline of silence, the power of listening, and thus the joy of learning.

37

When the *avatara* (the incarnation of God) arrives in this world, He appears to our vision as a person standing against the very element of time itself. Time is forced to a standstill as a result of the very gravitas of His presence. The darkness recedes. The Sun of Dharma illumines all the world. The demonic know the stark reality of God's power with more assurance than they know even their own subjective existence. The demonic tremble at His presence. The devotees rejoice. And reality itself bows at His feet. Victory is Bhagavan's alone.

38

The greatest offense (*guru-aparadha*) that we can commit against the *guru* is to arrogantly treat the *guru* as an ordinary person. The *guru* is not our buddy. The *guru* is not our colleague. The *guru* is not our therapist. The *guru* is not our employee. The true *guru* is the self-realized sage who will guide us away from our self-imposed illusion and toward the spiritual emancipation for which our innermost heart yearns. He smashes our illusion with the hammer of Truth. The true *guru* is our personal gateway to liberation. View the true *guru* through such eyes of devotion, dedication and faith, and you will advance quickly toward liberation.

39

At one time, during the Vedic era, human culture was designed to be a celebration of the beauty of spirit and of Truth. Such a Dharmic culture allows each individual to meet all their material and spiritual aspirations in an environment of freedom, positive encouragement, meaningful community and the highest quality of life. Let each one of us strive in every way to make such truly human culture a living reality once again. Let us strive to create a Dharma Nation, a nation that is guided by the eternal principles of Dharma. Dharma Rashtra Jayate.

40

In Sanatana Dharma, every earthly woman is understood to be a partial manifestation of the divine Shakti, the Goddess, and must be respected accordingly. Both the masculine and the feminine principles find their ultimate repose in the Absolute. Our women are meant to be respected, cherished, protected and loved. They must never be abused in any manner. To do so is to offend the Goddess. Aum Sri Maha Lakshmyai Namah.

41

Aum. All that is perceivable and conceivable has its very existence secured due solely to the sustaining presence of the Divine. If you could point to anything in which God were not immediately present, you would be pointing to nothing. Without God, there is nothing. Only with God is there everything. Aum.

42

Aum. Society and spirituality cannot be artificially separated. A society that neglects the crucial spiritual needs of its citizens is a society that has consequently failed its citizens. Only a Dharma civilization, a Dharma Nation, has the ability to secure both the material and the spiritual needs of its citizens. But of these, thc spiritual element constitutes the primary foundation of any healthy society. Seek the spiritual, and all else will follow.

43

The path of Dharma stresses the importance of life's qualitative attainments. Thus, the primary tasks of the Vedic state must be the cultivation of nobility of the spirit, and the attainment of real and abiding happiness among its people.

44

Any self-described *'guru'* who insists that he is an *avatara* (incarnation) of God, or who allows naive followers to worship him as an *avatara* of God, is not an authentic *guru*. Rather, he is only a megalomaniacal charlatan who will inevitably abuse his innocent disciples. Illusions of grandeur automatically leads to abuse just as readily as gasoline thrown into a fire leads to an inferno. If your *guru* claims to be God, he has then exposed himself to not even be worthy of being seen as a beginner on the spiritual path, what to speak of being a supposed Master! Such manipulative frauds have harmed the sacred reputation of Sanatana Dharma time and again, and must be rejected by all responsible spiritual seekers. It is the duty of the Vedic community to speak with one voice in denouncing such spiritual abuse. The true *guru* has the humility and wisdom to know that he is not an omni-competent being, but that he is merely a modest servant of God. To view oneself as such a humble servant of God is the highest spiritual attainment of all. Aum Tat Sat.

45

The ancient principle of Sri Guru is one of the most important institutions of Sanatana Dharma. It is through the grace and the teachings of a true *guru* that we are gifted with the strength and insight necessary to traverse the path to God in peace and assurance. It is precisely because the principle of Sri Guru is so important that it is incumbent upon all followers of Dharma to understand what a true *guru* is and what a true *guru* is not. A true *guru* has humility, compassion, wisdom and supremely ethical behavior. A true *guru* does not lie, abuse their disciples, engage in unethical behavior, or allow grandiose claims to be made about themselves by their disciples. Glories to the Sadguru - the true *guru*!

46

The quality of life must be the foremost of all concerns. Everything else in matters of governance, economics and social issues is secondary to this all-important quality of life directive. The overriding question that any good government or social system needs to ask is: '*Are the people of the nation actually happy*?' The answer to this question in almost nation upon the Earth today is that the people are not happy. Indeed, the people are miserable. Thus, most modern governments have failed their people. The time has now come to replace such failed governments with governments that will actually take their mandate to secure the people's wellbeing seriously. Such governing administrations can only be governments that are guided by the principles of Dharma in their policymaking.

47

Aum. Dharma seeks to establish human happiness, prosperity and meaningful progress through natural balance, a just order, peace and social harmony. Aum Tat Sat.

48

The ideal ruler is a natural born leader who personifies the dual qualities of administrative prowess, and advanced spiritual attainment. The greatest leader cannot merely have practical political wisdom alone; neither can he merely have spiritual insight alone. He must possess both simultaneously. He is a philosopher-king, a warrior-priest, a sage-ruler. He wields both the sword of state, and the sacred staff of the wise person. This is the Chakravartin, the perfect monarch. The Earth has been blessed with the divine presence and guidance of many such Chakravartins in the past. May we witness the rapid ascendency of such a Chakravartin soon again.

49

The personality of Nature contains different species, ecosystems, weather phenomena, laws of physics, etc. She is as deep and multifaceted as is any other person. Nature miraculously harmonizes the diverse elements of which She is composed in such a way as to create a greater integrated whole. Dharma, or Natural Law, reconciles seeming opposites, and integrates all the various elements of Nature, as well as of human nature, that might otherwise seem irreconcilable. Dharma is the harmony of diversity at its most spiritual and at its most meaningful of senses. It is only through Dharma that we fully grasp the wonder that is Nature.

50

Free will is one of the essential attributes of consciousness, of *atman*. All living beings are gifted with free will. There is no such thing as consciousness without free will. Having free will is central to what it means to be spiritual. Though we have temporarily placed ourselves under the temporary illusion of bondage to ego (*ahamkara*) and ignorance (*avidya*), this bound state is not our natural constitutional position. Spirit is free. We are ultimately designed to be free and to freely use our will to exercise good.

51

Part of what it means to exercise free will spiritually is to consciously use that will to work for Vedic justice, for a better world, and for Dharma. Sadly, all too many people today have accepted the stereotyped caricature of the spiritual person as being callously divorced from the concerns of this world. Nothing could be further from the truth. Historically, we have seen that the greatest leaders of society, and the most effective purveyors of positive change, have always been spiritual people. Totalitarianism, tyranny and fanaticism, in all their varied forms, represent the very opposite social-political philosophy of Dharma, and must always be vigorously fought in the name of Dharma. Many more contemporary *gurus*, Swamis and Acharyas should speak out boldly and strongly against any form of injustice in this world, in addition to their task of teaching the *siddhanta* (highest philosophical conclusion) of Vedanta and the path of Yoga. It is their duty to do so; and when they do not do so, they fail at their duty both ethically and spiritually.

52

Thoughtful followers of Dharma observe a strict lacto-vegetarian diet, a diet of compassion that seeks to reduce suffering to its minimal level possible. Such a diet means the complete avoidance of meat, fish and eggs. One must strive to be a vegetarian in order to be a truly compassionate and healthy *yogi*. To not be a vegetarian is to engage in a culture of death and suffering, and to thus harm yourself and others.

53

All living beings, regardless of their outward physical form, are *atman*, or individual units of consciousness, in their innermost essence. Learn to treat yourself as *atman*, and to treat others as *atman*, and love and justice will rule the Earth. Aum Hari Aum.

54

Depression, existential angst, and a deep sense of meaninglessness have overcome a large number of people in our present Age of Conflict (Kali Yuga). This present state has been brought about due to the systematic de-spiritualization of every aspect of human culture that has been instigated by the tiny, corrupt elite who presently controls our society. The ultimate cure for society's present crisis of depression and meaninglessness is for the people to begin to reverse this ongoing deconstruction of reality, and to re-embrace a life of meaning, a life of the spirit, a life of Dharma. Our greatest task today is to reconstruct a pure Vedic civilization. Let us work actively and practically to restore Dharma in our society and in our own lives. Let us make this a world of beauty and wellbeing once again.

55

Sanatana Dharma is a philosophy, a world-view and a way of life that is open to, and welcoming of, all qualified spiritual seekers without prejudice. Sanatana Dharma is not Indian, Eastern or Asian. It is the Eternal Natural Way. It is the heritage of all who are truly human (*manushya*). All qualified seekers are welcome into the family of Dharma. The only price for admission to that supreme realm of Truth is humility, sincerity, openness and eagerness.

56

The only valid alternative to the destructiveness of materialism, consumerism, and greed is a world-view and culture based upon authentic spirituality. Attempting to fight these destructive materialistic tendencies with only further materialism, such as with Marxism, atheism, capitalism, and socialism, is self-defeating. It is like attempting to stop a fire by hurling matches into it. We cannot fight the ravages of materialism with yet more materialism, but only with Dharma spirituality. Dharma spirituality is the only effective and true idealism of our age.

57

A Dharma Nationalist is a person who wants to see the organic principles of Dharma practically instantiated in political form in a modern nation-state. The only idealism that is truly effective, comprehensive, and worth fighting for is that idealism that works toward the creation of such a Dharma Nation. Dharma Nationalism is the political alternative of the future. Be a Dharma Nationalist. Build a Dharma Nation.

58

We are present in this world as human beings in order to transcend our merely human nature, and to re-embrace our true identity as eternal spiritual beings. The basis of the 'human' is the spiritual.

59

Ultimately, we are spiritual beings having a material experience. We are consciousness temporarily traversing the temporal realm. However, we do still have to respect both our spiritual and our material dimensions within their own ontological contexts. Yoga philosophy teaches that we must transcend our lower dimensions of body (*deha*), emotions (*abhitapa*), mind (*manas*), and intellect (*buddhi*), and false ego (*ahamkara*), and embrace our true essential state as spiritual beings (*atman*). But once we achieve this proper spiritual perspective, we can now understand and happily employ our material human (*manushya*) aspects in the service of soul (*atman*). This is why the sage has conquered false ego, but is still fully aware of his true identity; the sage transcends human intellect, but is still the wisest of all persons; the sage transcends the human mind, but still has the ability to penetrate reality like none other; the sage transcends emotions, but loves all beings; the sage transcends the body, but is a font of health and well-being. It is in transcending the merely human, and embracing the eternal, that the sage brings even the human vehicle to its ultimate perfection.

60

Our actual purpose, from a purely spiritual perspective, is to consciously live in reciprocal loving communion with God, and to reflect that love in our own being at every moment of our existence. While we are never truly separated from God, at the present moment we are under the illusion of such separation due to our choice to live in accordance with illusory ego (artificial self, or *ahamkara*) rather than in the higher interest of our true self, which is our soul (*atman*). Whether we are still embodied or existing completely free from bodily restrictions, the purpose of life is still the same: to think about, worship, love and meditate upon the Divine, Bhagavan Sri Krishna. Thus, when we find ourselves situated in perfectly instantiated devotional meditation (*bhakti*) upon God, we are situated in our life's true purpose. Aum Hari Aum.

61

An authentic spiritual teacher (*guru*) must exhibit deep humility, unwavering ethical behavior, honesty, a lack of greed, true knowledge based upon the wisdom of the Vedic scriptures, and respect for his or her students. Such characteristics mark the presence of a true and honorable *guru*. If any of these qualities are not present in a person, then that person is not a true and legitimate *guru*.

62

There is no living being who does not inherently seek. We come into this world seeking. Most leave this world still seeking. For most, the unknown goal of our search is never found. This is because our true search is not an outward search, but an inner one. Seek that goal which, once found, makes your seeking come to a natural end and gives you permanent fulfillment. That object of your seeking is God. Nothing else will ever truly fulfill you. Nothing.

63

Aum. In order to ensure the protection of all individual liberties, as well as the proper and smooth functioning of the state government itself, Natural Law calls for the absolute minimal amount of intrusive government necessary to ensure that the citizens are protected, secure, and educated. Perfect government ensures the people's welfare without hampering the people's innate right to freedom. When government oversteps its natural bounds and begins to intrude upon the rights of the people, that government has then become a tyranny, and no longer legitimately reflects the will of the people. Such tyrannical regimes have as their only true purpose their own inevitable replacement with a Dharmic government. Aum Tat Sat.

64

Aum. The ravages of secular-materialist modernity have severely distorted human culture and negated the life of the spirit. The Dharma world-view represents a positive moral and philosophical alternative to the many ills and cultural distortions of atheistic modernity. Vedic culture is human culture, because Vedic culture is the model of spiritual civilization. Aum.

65

Aum. Both prayer and meditation are important for a healthy and balanced spiritual life. Through prayer, we are communicating our concerns to God; and through meditation, we are allowing God to reveal Himself to us. Prayer is speaking to God. But meditation is listening humbly to God's response to our heart. Aum.

66

In the last several decades, a mercantile (*vaishya*) consciousness has overtaken much of the European and American Yoga community. The goal of too many Yoga teachers has been to imitate the business model rather than the traditional model of the Yoga-Mandira, or the sacred temple of Yoga practice. True Yoga, however, is not a profits-driven industry. It is not a business, or merely a way to gain fame, fortune and followers. The authentic practice of Yoga does not consist merely of having a good marketing plan, establishing the right type of corporate status, or out-maneuvering the competition. The ancient tradition of Yoga is the highest path for achieving self-realization and God-consciousness. It is the spiritual path par excellence. It forms the very essence of all true religion. It is Sanatana Dharma - the Eternal Natural Way. Thus, Yoga is in actuality a priceless gift.

67

Aum. Having a direct and sustained awareness of our eternal connection with the Absolute is the entire goal of the Yoga system in its pure and authentic form. This is known as *samadhi.* Aum Tat Sat.

68

The highest enlightened state achievable by the *yogi* is that state in which the *yogi's* consciousness is completely abiding in God. Abiding in God means cultivating God-consciousness with an attitude of complete surrender (*prapatti*), which is the ultimate goal of the path of Yoga.

69

In our contemporary materialistic world, we have developed a culture in which every desirable value, acceptable aspiration, and measure of success is assessed in purely quantitative terms, to the detriment of the deeper qualitative value of life's most cherished dimensions. Happiness, in today's culture, is determined by how much you have, and not by how deep is the joy you experience. Amount and quantity, however, are not synonymous with depth. Rather than endlessly increasing the quantity of temporary material things in our lives, Dharma stresses the importance of life's quality, the cultivation of nobility of the spirit, and the attainment of real and abiding happiness. When the focus is on quality, then appropriate quantity naturally follows with little effort.

70

The follower of Sanatana Dharma views nature as a manifestation of God's creative power and energy (*shakti*), and as being inherently good. The Dharmi (follower of Dharma) approaches nature with love and acceptance, and lives in intimate harmony and environmental integration with his natural surroundings. A large part of what it means to practice Yoga is to be in love with nature, and to yearn to be in nature whenever possible. Yogis, thus, yearn for pristine forested areas. To enjoy the full Yoga experience is to practice Yoga and meditation in nature.

71

Sanatana Dharma is the Eternal Natural Way. It is the origin and culmination of all true spirituality, philosophy, and yearning to know the higher Reality. Live in accordance with Dharma, and your heart and mind will be at peace.

72

Aum. Sanatana Dharma is an expression of the divine intelligence that naturally underlies the more empirical aspects of our cosmos. Sanatana Dharma is the underlying totality of all the eternal metaphysical principles that make even the subordinate laws of physical reality meaningful and operative. Without the metaphysical, there is no basis for the physical. Aum.

73

The greatest era in the history of Sanatana Dharma does not lay behind it, but is about to occur in our lifetime. Sanatana Dharma is not an archaic tradition of superstitions to be relegated to the past, but represents the most cutting-edge and spiritually advanced world-view that the earth has ever known. In the near future - in our very lifetime - we will witness all culture, religion, politics, arts, economics, sciences, and world thought being reshaped in the light of Dharma, in the light of the Eternal Natural Way. For this new compassionate and healthy Dharmic world to become a reality, however, all Dharmis (followers of Dharma) must exhibit the courage, the strength, the fearlessness, the humility, and the determination to dedicate ourselves wholly to practicing authentic Dharma, and to serving humanity with all of our being. Together, united in strength, purpose, and compassion, we can recreate our world for the better. May God empower us that we may revive Dharma in our world.

74

For followers of Yoga spirituality, all living creatures are considered to be worthy of respect, compassion and ethical concern, regardless of the temporary bodily form they may currently have. To the true *yogi*, a cow, an elephant, or a tree is as much an eternal living spirit (*atman*) as is a human being. A true *yogi* would no more eat a cow, a chicken, a pig, a fish, or any other living being than they would eat a human being. Aum Shanti.

75

Vegetarianism makes sense from an environmental, ethical, economic, political and spiritual perspective. A diet of death kills the spirit. It kills morality. It kills all true culture. But a diet of life elevates and liberates the spirit. Living a life of Dharma means following a diet of life. Celebrate life by following a healthy vegetarian diet. Aum Shanti.

76

Freedom is one of the most important natural qualities of the human spirit. Without freedom, we cease to be human. And without the right to both personal and national self-rule, human beings are not free. Dharma teaches that all historically defined peoples, linguistic groups, nations, tribes and races have the inherent human right to sovereign self-governance, and to enjoy the benefits of having their own autonomous and independent, culturally homogeneous states if they so choose.

77

When a people feel they have the freedom to express themselves and their aspirations within the liberating bounds of their own free nation, the consequent feelings of security and liberty that result naturally decreases the need for war and conflict. Liberty and tyranny are thoroughly juxtaposed concepts. Dharma sustains liberty. Dharma is freedom.

78

Aum. According to the principles of Bhakti Yoga (the Yoga of devotional consciousness), the heart of Yoga consists of the eternal dance between the lover (the soul) and the Beloved (God). In the illusory state imposed upon him by false ego, the soul feels himself to be artificially disconnected from God. Bhakti Yoga is the path that brings about the reunion of soul and God, and thus reinstates the soul to his natural state of eternal devotional consciousness toward the Supreme Godhead, Bhagavan Sri Krishna. Bhakti Yoga can only be successfully practiced under the expert guidance of a *shuddha-bhakta* Mahabhagavata, a qualified *guru* who is a pure devotee of God. Aum.

79

The quiet nurturing presence of the ancient gods and goddesses reminds us of the majestic grandeur of what once was. The direct experience of God, Whom even the ancient gods and goddesses worship as the very source of their own spiritual being, gives us the hope of what will be in eternity. We must honor the gods and goddesses always, but absorb our consciousness eternally within the Parameshvara, the highest God of all.

80

True spirituality transcends all forms of sectarianism, denominationalism, fanaticism, fundamentalism and unwarranted hatred. True spirituality knows only love, wisdom, innocence and beauty. Man-made religions come and go. They are institutions made of sand. True spirituality, on the other hand, is eternal. It is natural. It transcends all earthly institutions. True spirituality is the Eternal Natural Way - Sanatana Dharma.

81

Aum. We must cultivate four primary qualities in ourselves in order to know our true selves, and to know God. These are Humility, Sincerity, Openness to Guidance, and Deep Yearning to know and serve the Divine. To the depth and degree that you possess these four qualities, to that same measure will your path to God be clear. Hari Aum.

82

Aum. To always choose the upward path of nobility in all of your thoughts, words and deeds is to live in accordance with Dharma. The noble yogi and the warrior will always strive for nothing less than complete excellence in all things. The follower of Dharma strives always to be *arya*, noble. Aum Tat Sat.

83

Dharma Economics is thoroughly opposed to both economic extremes of Socialism and Capitalism. Both of these inherently flawed systems have arisen as a direct result of materialism, selfishness, envy and greed. Both systems exalt the importance of quantitative acquirement over the inherent qualities of human dignity and spiritual value. Both systems have dehumanized the individual person, and have turned the natural beauty and inherent value of the Earth into a devalued and lifeless commodity designed merely for selfish exploitation. The system of Dharma economics outlined in "*The Dharma Manifesto*" is the only viable alternative to such reckless economic materialism.

84

There is never a time when we are separated from God. There is only the illusion of separation due to our false ego. False ego is the artificial wall keeping the ever-present Divine Godhead from our current sight. In actuality, there is nowhere where God is not. There is never real separation from God. Deeply realize this truth, and you will know God here and now.

85

The goal of your life should be to live in such a manner that the Truth expresses itself through you in everything you think, speak and do. Your desire should be to develop a love of God that is so great - so humble - that when someone looks upon you, they see, not merely you, but that all-encompassing love alone. By your own living example, you should wish to teach, inspire and guide others to that very same Truth that so graciously transformed you. In this way, be a blessing always upon the lives of all you meet.

86

The state of *shanti*, peace, is much more than merely the negation of war or violence. True peace is the positive reality of experiencing our highest spiritual nature. Peace is an attribute of our soul; and our soul is an attribute of God, the ultimate source of peace. God is peace. To know peace, know God. Aum Shanti.

87

Dharma is living. We need to perfectly understand Dharma; to practice Dharma in our everyday lives; to be examples of Dharma for others to emulate; and in every way, to support those who have devoted their lives to teaching Dharma. It is in this way that we will personify Dharma in our being. This is living Dharma.

88

Every sector of our society has been fundamentally distorted by the unnatural encroachment of mercantile culture. The business mentality has thoroughly infected areas of cultural and even spiritual concern that were not previously seen as being ordinarily business oriented. Now, for example, even many false spiritual teachers and Yoga centers operate as businesses. The overriding paradigm and operating principle of all elements of culture has now become the business model. This has led to the systematic corruption of our people, to the devaluing of life, culture and nature, and to a warped sense of greed and selfishness in our people. This new 'mercantile culture' that has spiritually distorted our culture must be eliminated. Spiritual culture is - in its goals, methods and attitude - the very opposite of mercantile culture.

89

Veda, perfect knowledge, comes into visible being as a result of the direct, non-mediated insight into the nature of the Divine on the part of the enlightened sages (*rishis*). If you are to know Truth in its fullness of being, then you must access the Vedic scriptures and the teachings of the enlightened sages. A Sadguru (authentic spiritual master) is the living personification of the deepest purport of the Vedic scriptures. Learn at the feet of such a Sadguru with humility and sincerity, and your knowledge will be perfect.

90

Nature is not a scientific specimen. Nature is a living being, a mother, a woman, a Goddess, whom we are to love, respect and nurture - as she so patiently nurtures us. Whenever possible, practice meditation and Yoga deep within Nature, being lovingly enveloped by Her beauty, healing energies and grace. She will inspire and sustain you in your practice. She is a hidden, yet beautifully nurturing, *guru*.

91

Aum. Meditation consists of first stilling the fluctuations of the mind, and then awakening one's inner self to Transcendence. Only with a mind first at peace can we then have the ability to look within and to begin to meditate effectively upon the Divine. Aum.

92

My *guru* would often say that reciting the *mantra* Aum is like saying a tremendous "Yes!" to the cosmos. The cosmos has an inherent beauty. The source of that beauty is the presence of God in all things. Aum is the sound representation of this omnipresence of God. Aum is non-different from God.

93

Aum. Yoga means Union. This union is known in three ways: Union within our own very often fragmented being. It means union between ourselves and all beings who lay outside of ourselves. Most importantly, it means union between ourselves and God in the form of transcendental loving relationship. It is in steadfastly practicing Yoga spirituality that we can fully experience the essential unity and harmony of all things. Aum.

94

Dharma is a pre-religious spiritual phenomenon in both its essence and function. Dharma existed at a time before there were such manmade institutions as sects, or world religions. Dharma is the eternal essence of the universe. Thus, Dharma serves as the very basis of all true religion.

95

Spiritual experience must always be coupled with discernment (*viveka*), the ability to use our keen intellects and philosophical sense to separate truth from falsehood, the real from the apparent, light from dark, good from evil. The heart and intellect must always operate together. Philosophy is not sufficient for knowing Truth, but it is necessary. Only with such a healthy balance can we approach the Truth.

96

Dharma is the most reliable vehicle to satisfy the natural yearning that we have within to stretch our hearts and intellects beyond the known world, and to experience the source of all reality.

97

Aum. The true *guru* never insists that he is God. Rather, the true *guru* feels privileged to be a humble servant of the Divine. He acts always in the role of a humble servant of God. The sincere student must, in turn, humbly and submissively approach such a true *guru* for expert guidance and instruction, and view himself as the humble servant of the true *guru.* With such a pure soul as his guide, the sincere student too will eventually be worthy to view himself as a humble servant of God. Aum Tat Sat.

98

Take shelter in the association of other good, sincere and spiritually oriented people. Firmly reject the association of those who are dark, selfish, destructive, and in ignorance. It is in the familial embrace of our Dharma community that we deepen our love for God and for each other. This is the meaning of *satsangha*, association with the good.

99

Aum Hari Aum. Due to having its originating source in the Divine, the Name of God (*hari-nama*) intimately participates in the essence of the Divine. The Name of God is, thus, non-different from God Himself. Meditate on the divine Names of God in *mantra* form if you wish to know God directly and immediately. *Aum Namo Narayanaya* is the highest of such *mantras*.

100

Aum. To surrender to the illusion of false ego is our greatest bondage. To surrender to the reality of God is our greatest freedom. All beings without exception need to surrender to one or the other, either illusion or God. Chose to surrender to that which will make you free. Aum.

101

Dharma Economics favors an economic system that is localized, values-based, spiritually centered, and that fosters the wondrous engine of individual human creativity without destroying the inherent good of the human spirit and of the Earth. Positive economic growth meets people's essential needs without encouraging the poisonous excesses of greed and selfishness. Dharma completely favors the development of small-scale, localized free enterprise and small businesses, as well as economic policies that will encourage the unbridled unleashing of the individual person's creative potential. Dharma is, however, opposed to the creation of large-scale, impersonal, multinational corporatism. The demonic ideologies of both Socialism and Capitalism are thus at odds with the natural way. Vedic philosophy, thus, rejects both Socialism and Capitalism in favor of an economics that is based upon the natural, justice and freedom.

102

Yoga can only be practiced in a state of *sattva* (goodness). Sattvika consciousness - the state of goodness, purity, cleanliness, integral health and light - is best cultivated by leading a life that is natural, spiritual, organic, virtuous and pure in every aspect. *Sattva* leads to *shuddha-sattva* (transcendent goodness). The states of *rajas* (passion) and *tamas* (darkness) only lead to the very opposite of the spiritual.

103

Aum Hari Aum. Such is the just and impartial nature of the law of *karma*: If we wish to be treated justly, then we must treat others, likewise, with justice. If we are not just, then we cannot expect justice to be extended toward us. Aum Shanti.

104

A society that neglects the crucial spiritual needs of its citizens, and that is incapable of celebrating the Transcendent foundation of reality, is a society that is inherently dysfunctional, and that has consequently failed its citizens. A Dharmic government would overtly acknowledge and celebrate the Transcendent as the very foundation upon which all government must be based, and as the primary source of legitimacy of any and all governmental authority. Evam Bhavatu. May it be so.

105

The idea of Karma Yoga is to make our everyday activities into an active meditation through which we can focus on God, even as we perform our day-to-day tasks. We must meditate on God as we cook, as we eat, as we drive, as we study, and as we work. With the practice of Karma Yoga, we transcend the creation of materialistic *karma* by transcendentalizing our everyday activities. We learn how to keep our consciousness ever focused upon the Divine, and to thus know perfection.

106

The *Bhagavad Gita* teaches us that there are three paths of action that a person can potentially follow. These are the paths of Exploitation, Renunciation or Dedication. With exploitation, we selfishly exploit the things of this material world, live only to please ourselves, and in this way produce karmic effects that keep us bound to our present state of ignorance (*avidya*). With renunciation, on the other hand, we artificially reject all action in this world, and try to lead the extreme life of an ascetic. This is a lifestyle that is especially impractical in this day and age. Both the paths of exploitation and renunciation are opposite extremes. But with a consciousness of dedication (or Karma Yoga), on the other hand, we perform all of our activities - cooking, cleaning, work, rest - in a spirit of meditative dedication to the Absolute. In this way, we are not producing *karma*, and more positively we are refining and spiritualizing our consciousness. Reject the extreme paths of exploitation and renunciation, and embrace the healthy path of dedication.

107

Both knowledge and practice (*sadhana*) are of great importance in spiritual life. They are the two wings of the eagle. If the eagle is lacking either wing, she will not be able to fly. Cultivate philosophical knowledge while simultaneously practicing spirituality with dedication. In this balanced way, you will directly know and experience truth.

108

Real progress means elimination of that which is destructive and untrue, coupled with the new acceptance of that which is conducive to meaningful growth and true. We cannot know what to eliminate from our lives as obstacles and negative psychic patterns (*anarthas*) if we do not take the time to look within. Looking within takes incredible courage, and a willingness to accept what we discover about ourselves. It also requires the patience and humility to accept what we see and want to then change, because what we see will often be a challenge to our egoic sense of self. This is the slow, steady work necessary to make meaningful and real progress on the path toward God. This is *sadhana* - spiritual practice.

109

Spiritual liberation proceeds through the two successive stages of a) self-realization, and then b) God-consciousness. The first goal of the spiritual path is self-realization (*atma-jnana*), since we can know nothing at all unless we first know ourselves. We must first know the knower. Only then do we proceed to God-consciousness (*brahma-vidya*), because even our true self has an ultimate source. God is the final place of rest, peace, joy and wholeness. God is the ultimate home of the soul.

110

Life does have a purpose, however hidden from view that purpose might sometimes seem to us. There is, indeed, a hidden beauty behind all things, if we only have the eyes to see it. Most people today are traversing this earth like the blind, never seeing the light, crashing violently into one another, hurting themselves and those around them, unable to appreciate the beauty that they are constantly surrounded by. A small number of people, however, are much less blind than others. Some can see things clearly that others cannot see at all. To such people of true spiritual vision, even the water, the Earth, the wind or nature can become the vehicle through which God's loving whisper is revealed. It is in the consistent practice of meditation that we develop the ears to hear that whisper and the eyes to see the beauty. This is why vividly experiencing the presence of God is called *darshana*, or 'to see'.

111

The concept of liberation (*moksha*) in Sanatana Dharma is very different from the Judeo-Christian concept of 'heaven'. Liberation is not a geographically situated terrain. Rather, *moksha* implies the complete and radical existential freedom of the human person, consisting in qualitative oneness with the Absolute (Brahman). Such a state of liberation is experienced in the form of ecstatic bliss without limit. We can experience the liberated state of *moksha* even while still situated within the material world. *Moksha* is not a place. It is a state of consciousness. It is within us all.

112

Giving of ourselves in spiritual service (*seva*) to help save the world is not something that we should ever feel is a burden or something that should give us the right to be even more egotistical. It is actually the greatest privilege that we could ever have and a blessing from God when we are given the opportunity to serve Dharma. *Seva* should be our Dharma. Spiritual service toward God and *guru* should be our very way of being.

113

The preliminary goal of Yoga is to have a controlled mind. Having a manic, unfocused and flighty mind is the polar opposite of having a mind situated in Yoga. First control the fluctuations of the mind. Have a mind that is calm, peaceful, focused, deliberative and as deeply tranquil as a beautiful, refreshing lake. Only with such a controlled mind will you be able to focus your meditative awareness fully on the Divine, and thus know first-hand the incalculable rewards of spiritual life.

114

Aum. To help another person deepen their knowledge and experience of God is what it means to show true love toward that person. This is the highest of all benevolence. Helping someone spiritually is the most meaningful form of compassion. Aum.

115

The true *guru* always challenges the student in various ways to encourage the student's sincerity, discipline and determination. Not every student passes such spiritual tests. Such is the nature of all tests that not everyone guaranteed success. For the wise student, however, such tests are always understood to be the greatest of blessings. Deep sincerity alone always leads to success in all spiritual tests.

116

Aum Namo Narayanaya. The scriptures of Sanatana Dharma are clear that Narayana, or Krishna, is the one and only Supreme Being. Brahma was created by Narayana in order to be the architect of the material universe. Moreover, Shiva is himself created by Brahma. All the other gods and goddess are subservient to Narayana, Brahma and Shiva. Narayana alone is uncreated, eternal, and transcends all materiality and illusion. Narayana is the source of all. The supreme status of Narayana as God is confirmed in all the major scriptures of Sanatana Dharma, including the *Vedas*, *Ramayana*, *Mahabharata*, *Bhagavad Gita,* the *Puranas*, *Upanishads*, etc. The scriptures proclaim with one united and unequivocal voice that devotional consciousness (*bhakti*) toward Narayana is the highest path to spiritual liberation. Jaya Sriman Narayana.

117

Spiritual egotism is often mistaken for true spirituality. The two, however, could not be more different from one other. Spiritual egotism is the very last trap that the illusory ego imposes upon the bound living being. Spiritual egotism is the futile attempt to use spirituality and religion for one's own materialistic gains, and is thus nothing more than an extension of selfishness into the religious sphere. It becomes manifest in the form of fanaticism, dogmatism, showmanship, the misuse of yogic techniques for psychic and mystical attainments, using spirituality to cheat others or to obtain sensual gratification, or taking a shallow and self-serving approach to spirituality. True spirituality, on the other hand, has self-transcendence and devotional service toward God as its goal. Authentic spirituality cultivates humility, meaningful compassion, equanimity and peace of mind, as well as goodness and morality in the sincere practitioner. We must practice pure spirituality, and not spiritual egotism, if we wish to attain the highest goal.

118

Great goodness often draws evil inadvertently upon itself. This is the case because evil people are by nature envious, ego-driven, and falsely threatened by the light of good people. They cannot comprehend the powerful tranquility of the soul who is surrendered to the Divine. It is for this reason that great sages and saints have often been persecuted throughout history by individuals who possess a psychopathic nature. Wherever we find the good, including in our own selves, we must defend it with unyielding strength and courage. Wherever we see evil, we must annihilate it without remorse, hesitation or weakness. This is how we defend Dharma. Thus will we be worthy of our human birth.

119

You become like that upon which you meditate. This is one of the most powerful and transformative psychological principles of Yoga spirituality and of Dharma. Objects of meditation are not all the same. What you choose to meditate upon does matter. If you focus your concentrated awareness upon negative, dark and evil things, you will become likewise. If you focus your devotional awareness on evil beings, corrupt politicians, and demonic entities, you will become like them. If you focus upon ghosts and spirits, your inner being will be deeply haunted by such beings. If, on the other hand, you focus your concentrated awareness upon the positive, light and goodness, then you will know these in your life. If you place your meditative thoughts upon angelic beings, the gods and goddesses, your mind and psyche will become elevated and tranquil. If you place your devotional meditative awareness on God, the source of all good things, then your mind, thoughts, heart and soul will know the very highest bliss of spiritual freedom. Choose to meditate always upon the very highest source of all good things. That highest of all good is the Supreme Godhead, Bhagavan Sri Krishna.

120

Socialism is the celebration of weakness and envy. Capitalism is the celebration of callousness and greed. Dharma represents the thorough rejection of both of these falsely proffered, materialistic dichotomies. Dharma teaches us how to be strong and self-reliant, while simultaneously being giving and compassionate toward others. The science of Dharma economics accesses the ancient laws of nature and uses those principles in the modern era to give people full prosperity, health, peace, justice and order. Dharma is the third alternative to both class envy and exploitation. It is opposed to the abusive systems of both Socialism and Capitalism.

121

A true *yogi* does not poison his body, mind and spirit with such intoxicating substances as alcohol, marijuana, cigarettes, ayahuasca or any other mind-altering drug. Such harmful drugs deeply ruin the psyche, diminish inner strength, open one's mind to dark influences, and lead to a mind that is incapable of the sharpness, discernment and focus necessary to lead a life of wisdom and virtue. The fallen *yogi* is seeking to obscure Reality by abusing intoxicants, and is thus only a *yogi* for show. The true *yogi*, on the other hand, is seeking a clear and vivid vision of Reality. Choose to be a true *yogi*, and you will achieve the greatest goal of Yoga.

122

Whatever information that enters our lives which is contrived, derived artificially, falsely perceived, or grounded in the propaganda of the demonic rulers of our materialistic society is the very opposite of Dharma. Always question the propaganda of the mainstream media, of the biased academic realm, of popular entertainment, and of self-serving politicians. Always seek instead that information which is derived from natural and organic sources, and that is based upon your own clearly perceived common sense if you want to know the reality of the world around you. Always use and trust your own discernment and discrimination over and above any artificially contrived messages. To discern and to discriminate is to be wise.

123

Though Yoga is a path that is open to everyone, not everyone can truly follow this path to its successful conclusion. Yoga is a discipline, a world-view, a philosophical system and a spiritual path that, while open to all, only reveals its most precious secrets to those few persons who approach it with sincerity, humility, discernment, discipline and the grace of the *guru*. Only that person who can approach the path of Yoga with such a dedicated mindset can achieve success, and thus has the full right to call himself a true *yogi*.

124

If you have it within your power, choose to live in a place that is most conducive to healthy living and spiritual advancement. Such places are called sattvic, or healthy, natural, pure and good. The rural countryside is the most sattvic of all places to reside. Such places are generally healthy, peaceful, natural, positive, life affirming, and supportive to a clear and uncorrupted mind. If you want to live in an area that is most conducive for spiritual growth, then live is such an area where you are close to nature, trees, forests, animals, clean air and water, as well as peace, quiet and solitude. The suburbs and city outskirts, on the other hand, are generally rajasic - they are passionate, hyperactive, materialistic and spiritually shallow. If possible, a *yogi* should not live in such rajasic places unless there is no choice. Finally, the inner city ghettos are tamasic in nature - they are dark, negative, lethargic, ignorant and spiritually enervating. Such tamasic areas are to be avoided completely by any serious *yogi.* It is almost impossible to be a successful *yogi* in the inner city. Our inner world is strongly affected by our external surroundings. Live in a place of goodness if you wish to cultivate goodness within yourself.

125

True equality can never be known in the material world. No two people are the same. No one person is ever fully equal to any other person. It is precisely in the uniquely individual variations between people that beauty, interestingness, and distinctiveness are seen. Nature is inherently variegated. Thus, to attempt to artificially impose equality where none is possible or necessary is to encourage a state of illusion and untruth. We are all blessed by God to be different from one another, with our own individual preferences, talents, capabilities and constitutional makeups. These natural differences between individuals are meant to be celebrated and used to their full capacity for the greater good. Each unique individual is to be recognized and respected in their dissimilitude from others. This is the way of nature - of Dharma. It is only on the transcendent, purely spiritual level that all living beings are truly equal. On the spiritual level, all living beings are eternal souls (*atman*), and finite reflections of the Infinite Divine. Only the liberated sage has the ability to see all living beings with such spiritually meaningful equal vision.

126

Sincerity is reflected in the honesty, trust, and patience with which we approach the spiritual path. Without such sincerity, there is no real spiritual progress along the path. It is in cultivating such sincerity that we will achieve enlightenment.

127

Jesus was not a Christian. Jesus was a Dharma Master and an accomplished *yogi*. He fully understood the Dharmic teaching on the omnipresence of the Divine. He understood that there is nowhere where God is not. It is, in fact, God's presence in all things that gives all things their very existence, reality and being. This is why one of God's designations is Sat - or 'being itself.' Jesus knew this and taught this to those who had the ears to hear. He was therefore a liberated sage and world teacher (*jagad-guru*).

128

There is nothing as disturbing and as damaging to the sanctity and reputation of Sanatana Dharma as when a false *'guru'* takes advantage of his innocent disciples and abuses them sexually, financially, emotionally, psychologically or physically. Just as disturbing is a fraudulent *'guru'* who makes the absurd claim to be God. There is zero excuse for such spiritually devastating behavior on the part of such pseudo-spiritual monsters. Such frauds are not practicing esoteric *'tantra'*, nor are they operating from a supposed realm 'beyond good and evil'. They have not 'transcended morality.' They are just narcissistic sociopaths who have chosen to abuse others. And when such abuse happens, true devotees of Dharma everywhere must speak out forcefully against such corrupt persons without trying to manufacture excuses for the fraudulent spiritual teacher. We must side immediately with the victims of such abuse, and must renew our own efforts to keep the Dharma community safe and free of such abuse. May Bhagavan protect us always from such demonic individuals in the cynical guise of *gurus*. Aum Namo Bhagavate Narasimhaya.

129

The true *guru* only comes to those who are blessed by God, and who have proven themselves ready to receive guidance with great humility. To have even had the opportunity to be in the presence of an authentic *guru* briefly in this lifetime means that one has accumulated tremendous *sukriti*, or spiritual blessings, in previous lifetimes. Understand the rare gift that it is to come into contact with such a pure *guru*. Listen quietly, respectfully and sincerely to the untainted words of such a genuine *guru*, and allow yourself to perfectly learn and deeply absorb his teachings unto you. Make yourself worthy of such a gift. For the *guru's* teachings are the greatest of all gifts. It is only to the direct degree that you approach the *guru* in this grateful and reverential manner that you will benefit from the *guru's* presence.

130

The concept of *ahimsa* is often mistaken in some spiritual circles as being a dogma of pacifism or as being an extremely impractical approach to non-violence. But the concept of ahimsa is not impractical. It is recognized that absolute non-violence is an impossibility within the material realm. We sometimes need to employ violence, for example, in order to uphold justice, to defend the innocent, and to punish the demonic. Also, as living beings, we all need to consume other living beings to survive, even if those other living beings are in the form plants. One important way that we express true *ahimsa* is by becoming vegetarians, even though vegetables and plant life, too, are still considered to be living beings. While they are indeed alive, they feel pain to a considerably lesser extent than do other, more mobile, beings. Thus, what *ahimsa* actually does ask of us is to always do everything within our power to minimize harm in everything that we think, say and do. Thus, even vegetarians are still engaging in some form of violence - but to the minimal extent possible. This same principle of the minimization of violence also applies to every other walk of life. As long as we are making a sincere attempt to minimize violence in all our activities, then we are following the principle of *ahimsa* perfectly. Aum Shanti.

131

The *yogi* who faithfully practices *ahimsa* (the minimization of harm) and vegetarianism learns empathy, compassion, and what the *Bhagavad Gita* calls *sama-darshina*, or 'equal vision' toward all living beings. He understands that all sentient beings are ultimately *atman* - pure consciousness. He comes to the realization that we are all spiritually connected, because we all share the same source in the Divine. Thus, the practice of *ahimsa* and vegetarianism is necessary to the process of full enlightenment. There is no enlightenment without following *ahimsa* and vegetarianism.

132

At one time in the historic past, previous to the commencement of the modern era, human culture was ordained by the gods to be a celebration of the beauty of spirit and of the transformative power of Truth. Such was the civilizational basis of Vedic society. In our current era, our corrupt leaders have purposefully abandoned this positive spiritual approach to culture and have, instead, transformed our modern societies into tyrannical landscapes devoid of meaning, freedom and beauty. Thus, the people suffer. Let each one of us strive in every way to make spiritual culture a living reality once again, even in the midst of our present Age of Conflict, the Kali Yuga. Let us re-establish Vedic civilization today. Aum Tat Sat.

133

Sriman-Narayana is the Supreme Godhead of Sanatana Dharma. The word 'Sriman' indicates the all-auspicious, feminine aspect of God as Sri Lakshmi Devi. The term 'Narayana' indicates the masculine aspect of God as the sustainer of all beings. They are two, as God/Goddess, and yet they are One as the Supreme Godhead. God is the Infinitely Auspicious Sustainer. Such is the ultimate nature of the Absolute. Jaya Sriman Narayana.

134

Our world is not without meaning. Our future is not without hope. Though the darkness of the Kali Yuga (our current 'Age of Conflict') and a resultant civilizational crisis has now descended upon us, the Sun of Dharma will soon be seen again. There is no cloud that can obscure our vision of the Sun forever. We will live to see the Sun of Dharma triumphant again, and to see a Golden Age of compassion, true culture, and the Natural Way be firmly reestablished. The International Sanatana Dharma Society is the movement that will bring about such a restoration of Dharma in the world today.

135

Each one of us needs healing in our lives on one level or another, and to one degree or another. In addition, our larger society and culture currently needs deep healing. Our mother, the Earth, Herself presently needs to be healed on a cosmic scale from the incessant abuse that corrupt politicians have leveled against Her. The only true healing, however, is that healing that occurs on the deepest of levels, on the spiritual level. To foster true healing, we must access the spiritual. We must live in accordance with Dharma.

136

Vedanta is the philosophical culmination of the Vedic path. It is the most advanced manifestation of wisdom available in any spiritual tradition on Earth. In Vedanta philosophy, the primary term for God is Brahman. All of reality has its original source in Brahman. All of reality has its grounding sustenance in Brahman. It is in Brahman that all of reality has its ultimate repose and purpose. The path of Sanatana Dharma is consciously and exclusively aiming toward this transcendent Absolute that is termed Brahman. The more personal name for Brahman in Sanskrit is Sriman Narayana. Sriman Narayana is Brahman. It is in devotional consciousness of Sriman Narayana that we achieve Brahma-vidya (God-Consciousness, realization of Brahman) and that we reach the perfection of our lives. *Satyam jnanam anantam brahma.*

137

Ego and envy emit a pronounced state of ugliness in anyone who has these negative traits. They produce a palpable ugliness that no amount of cosmetics, working out, or false façades can ever truly hide. Narcissism is ugliness. On the other hand, a spiritual attitude of humility, sincerity and devotion is a source of undeniable beauty for anyone who possesses these positive qualities. A spiritual person is a radiant person. There is no living being who is as beautiful as that person who is fully devoted to the highest source of all beauty, Sriman Narayana. That highest Absolute is the source of all lasting beauty. If you truly wish to know the Divine, then follow the path of true spiritual beauty. In this way, you will manifest true beauty in your life.

138

Meaningful communication with others is always a two-way process. We speak, but then we must also listen to the other person's response. This principle is true also in how we commune with the Divine. It is through prayer that we share our thoughts, concerns and praise with God. But it is in the stillness and silence of meditation that we allow ourselves to experience God's response within the temple of our hearts. Still your mind in meditation, and open yourself to God's grace. Do not be afraid to listen.

139

There are three cosmic activities, and three corresponding modes of energy. Creation is a reflection of the energy of passion (*rajas*). Destruction represents ignorance and darkness (*tamas*). But preservation is a manifestation of intelligence, strength and goodness (*sattva*). Preservation and *sattva* are the highest of these three activities and their corresponding modes (*gunas*). Preservation of Dharma, of that which is good, civilized, noble and spiritual, is the most difficult, and the most important, of all three activities.

140

The very heart of all spirituality consists of experiencing a direct and intimate realization of God in devotional consciousness (*bhakti*). It is such a direct experience that brings spirituality to life and that yields the sweetness of the Divine. Without such an experience of the Divine, spirituality is rendered devoid of all ultimate meaning and purpose. Spirituality thus becomes mere religion if it is missing direct experience.

141

God truly is that than which nothing greater can be conceived. God is beyond all human speculation. How then can we know God, however, if God is beyond all human speculation? The answer to this important question is that we can know God via *shabda*, or transcendental sound vibration. We can know God through God's own divine words in the form of the teachings of the liberated *rishis* (seers) who have directly experienced God, and through the Vedic scriptures, which are the literary records of those direct realizations. If we are not willing to trust the very words of God Himself on who and what is the Parabrahman, the Supreme Godhead, then we have not even begun our journey. To trust the words of the Divine is the very beginning of our path toward Truth.

142

It is in our intentional effort, and not merely our physical activity, that we realize spiritual advancement while performing *seva* (service) toward God. *Seva* is to be performed with an attitude of selfless love and humble dedication. If during our active service (*seva*) toward God our attitude is that we are somehow doing God a favor, or that we should be rewarded, then we are actually only doing ourselves and God a disservice. Service toward God is never to be seen as a burden, but as our greatest privilege and honor.

143

Many people in the modern Western world begin the practice of meditation with the goal of relieving stress and anxiety. This is very understandable since the many burdens of our modern materialist society necessarily leads to a tremendous amount of unnatural stress within people. Meditation is the very best stress-relieving program that exists. Mere physical and mental relaxation alone, however, is not the true aim of meditation. Relaxation affects us only on the levels of the physical and the mental. However, we are not our bodies or our minds. True meditation occurs on the transcendental, spiritual level - on the level of pure consciousness. It is only when we are in meditation with awareness of nothing but pure consciousness that we are truly meditating. Meditation that involves cultivating devotional consciousness toward the Supreme Godhead is especially to be understood to be the highest form of meditation. The most transcendental form of meditation that we can practice is meditation upon the *mantra* Aum Namo Narayanaya.

144

The Greek term '*philo-sophia*', from whence we derive the word 'philosophy', means '*love of wisdom*'. Thus, philosophy in its most essential form is not merely an intellectual exercise alone. It is not merely the study of an academic topic. Philosophy is not just one's subjective opinion, or an outlining of one's personal world-view. Rather, philosophy illumines the mind with the light of eternal Truth. True philosophy is expressed in the form of a spiritually motivated practice of discernment, coupled with the cultivation of devotional consciousness (*bhakti*), eventually leading to a direct and operative experience of the illuminating power of wisdom. True philosophy is a perfect balance of the head and the heart, of wisdom and of love. The true philosopher is, thus, the lover of God.

145

One of the most important ethical practices of Vedic spirituality is the extension of great compassion (*mahakaruna*) toward all sentient beings. Though there are many ways to show compassion, the most effective way that we can show compassion toward others is to help them spiritually. We must help others to know who they truly are within, and help them realize that they can live a life of unending bliss and joy. We must share Dharma with the world.

146

This is our fundamental problem. While the loving presence of the Divine is situated everywhere, we are often not even aware of the Divine being anywhere. That is the destructive power of our ego. That is power of our illusion. We are at all times being bathed in the loving ocean of God's grace, and yet we think that we are alone. More powerful than our illusion, however, is the power of Divine Grace. It is by that grace, we can experience the presence of the Divine in our daily life. We open ourselves to that divine grace through the systematic practice of Yoga and meditation. Aum Tat Sat.

147

A spirituality that is not practiced is a spirituality that is better left alone. Only a living spirituality has true meaning. Practice spirituality every moment of your life.

148

True spirituality must never be used as an excuse for self-indulgence. Such self-indulgence in the name of spirituality is, unfortunately, the foundation of most New Age thought and practice. True spirituality is neither merely a convenient source of income, nor a vehicle to be used for inflating our ego to even more monstrous proportions than they already are. True spirituality is never used. It is surrendered to. For true spirituality is the grace (*prasada*) of God. We must make ourselves worthy of that grace. We must abandon all modern New Age consumerism, and embrace the truly ancient and authentic wisdom traditions of our ancestors. Only with such an approach of sincerity and humility can we truly understand the deepest meaning of the spiritual.

149

An atheist is someone who falsely projects the source of his own experience of suffering onto a purportedly non-existent villain in the sky. The atheist cannot admit the fact that he is himself the source of his own suffering…and that he is also the potential source of his own enlightenment. Thus the atheist blames a god that he claims that does not even believe in. The atheist is simply a person who is in pain, and who does not possess the knowledge, the sincerity, or the humility to cope with it.

150

In spiritual life, we are called upon to embrace our inherent state of spiritual innocence. Innocence is expressed in having complete openness to the beauty and the wonder of God's creation. It is the very opposite of self-calculating narcissism. Being innocent, however, is not to be confused with being naïve. Innocence opens us to God's grace. Naïveté, on the other hand, opens us to illusion and to the possibility of cruel exploitation at the hands of the demonic. We avoid the pitfall of naïveté by cultivating sharp philosophical discernment (*jnana-viveka*) under the guidance of a qualified and authentic *guru*.

151

Any truth that is beyond knowing is a truth that is not worth being known. Thus, while it is a fact that God is *that than which nothing greater can be known*, we must never use God's inconceivability as an excuse to say that God cannot be known to us. Truth can be known, but only by the grace of Truth itself. The Infinite can only truly be claimed to be the Infinite if it contains within Itself the ability to make Itself known to the finite. Seek the Absolute, and you will know the Absolute by the grace of the Absolute. Athato Brahma Jijnasa.

152

The ruinous practice of usury (loaning money at an exorbitant interest rate) is an anti-Dharmic practice. It is an evil system that depletes human resources and creativity from hardworking people and from society. It degenerates healthy economic organisms into economies that are based upon debt slavery. Usury is the height of selfish exploitation, and has traditionally been rendered illegal by any and all Vedic governments and societies. This avaricious practice must be outlawed by all nations today. Dharma is opposed to all instances of usury.

153

From the perspective of Vedic philosophy, Marxism is understood to be an anti-Dharmic world-view (a *nastika* or *avaidika* dogma in Sanskrit). It is a thoroughly demonic ideology (*asura-vada*). The Marxist world-view has been one of the most detrimental factors responsible for reducing the spiritual beauty and glory of all traditional cultures throughout the globe to ashes everywhere its evil influence has touched. Marxism, in all its anti-human and anti-Dharmic manifestations, in both its overt and hidden forms, must be decisively defeated by those who wish to uphold Dharma. Dharma will be triumphant over all demonic forces.

154

Sanatana Dharma and Yoga are synonymous terms for the exact same path. Sanatana Dharma is Yoga in the form of the Natural Law that upholds reality. Yoga, on the other hand, is Sanatana Dharma in practiced application. Sanatana Dharma is the spiritual philosophy, and Yoga is the spiritual technique that gives meaning to the philosophy. Dharma and Yoga are one and the same path, and must be understood together for either to have effective meaning. If you are either a Dharmi who does not practice Yoga, or a *yogi* who does not also embrace Dharma, then you are akin to an eagle trying to soar toward the loftiest heights with the use of only one wing. To traverse to the highest realm, you must fly with the two powerful wings of Dharma and Yoga together.

155

We can never be truly separated from our divine Source. God is always with us, and we are always with God. We can, however, experience the illusion of separation from our Source due to the arising of false ego (*ahamkara*) as a covering and illusory mechanism. The ultimate goal of Yoga, meditation, Dharma, and of all authentic spiritual pursuits is to eliminate that illusion of separation that is caused by our false ego, and to once again experience our eternal, ecstatic union with the Divine. God is with us. We have only temporarily forgotten this fact.

156

We have a personal duty to Dharma to defend spiritual reality and to honor Truth in all spheres of human endeavor. When we uphold Dharma with our practical efforts, then we too are sustained by Dharma. In this way, we show our gratitude and dedication toward the divine gift of Dharma in our lives.

157

As within, so without. One's inner identity dictates one's outer behavior. If we false identify with our false, egoic self, then we are a burden upon all those who know us. But if we identify with our natural, spiritual self, then we will act in a spiritually whole and healthy way. We are then a blessing to all who know us. Always strive to be a blessing upon all sentient beings.

158

Once we have experienced Sriman Narayana (the Auspicious Sustainer) intimately, and have tasted deeply the sweet presence of God in our lives on a consistent basis through dedicated, devotional meditation (*bhakti*), we have then accessed the source of all Reality. All achievements that are truly worth having will then lay like jewels at our feet. When we have God, we have everything. Jaya Sriman Narayana.

159

It is in practicing a full and authentic yogic lifestyle that you will achieve true and meaningful happiness. Read the Vedic scriptures regularly, meditate daily on the divine names of Sriman Narayana (especially upon the *mantra* Aum Namo Narayanaya), practice the full, eightfold (*ashtanga*) system of Yoga spirituality, be a good and ethical person without excuses. Do all this, and you will eventually know the enlightened state of being. You will know spiritual liberation.

160

More often than not, wisdom is derived not from speaking, but from not speaking.

161

It is a myth that we must abandon the intellect in order to pursue spirituality. Quite the opposite, in fact, is the case. Attempting to progress spiritually without the benefit of one's natural intellectual faculties (*vichara*) and discrimination (*viveka*) is like trying to navigate the deepest and darkest cavern without the use of a lamp. The wisdom of discernment is our light on the path of Truth.

162

Let it not be your goal in life to be a mere intellectual. Rather, aspire to be intelligent. To be an intellectual is merely to amuse oneself with speculative facts and data. An intellectual attempts to know the taste of honey by licking the outside of the jar without ever opening the jar to actually taste the contents within. To be intelligent, on the other hand, is to enjoy a life of purpose that is guided by wisdom. The spiritually intelligent person has tasted deeply of the sweet honey of the Divine.

163

Nature represents the beauty of God manifest in the material world in such a way that all can experience His loving presence. Like God, Who is nature's source, nature is a place of beauty, healing, wholeness, harmony and well-being. Nature's deepest forests are in actuality lofty temples; but only if we have the eyes to see. It is especially when we meditate and practice Yoga deeply in nature, with our senses surrounded by her life-giving fragrance, that we can feel the presence God's beauty the most vividly. Make nature your temple, your Yoga center, and your home.

164

Meditation should be a part of everyday life. It should be non-distinct from our daily activities within the temporal world. We can potentially be in a meditative state of awareness even while eating, cooking, cleaning, working, or doing many very normal and necessary activities. Such active meditation within the context of our daily lives is known in Sanskrit as the path of Karma Yoga, or meditation in action. The essential practice is that we must always try to be situated in a consciousness of dedication and devotion to Sriman Narayana (the Supreme Godhead) while we do everything and anything, instead of being situated in a demeaned consciousness of exploitation. This is the nature of God-consciousness, that we remain aware of God's presence at all times and in all circumstances.

165

The only way to practice and truly benefit from Dharma spirituality is to practice Dharma on its own sacred terms. To insist on practicing Dharma only in a manner that is convenient or comfortable to us is merely an attempt to exploit Dharma as a further extension of our illusory ego (*ahamkara*) or selfish desires. Do not attempt to use Dharma. Rather, surrender your life to Dharma. To be an instrument in the sacred hands of Dharma is the greatest privilege that a living being can be gifted with.

166

Our religion is known in the Sanskrit language as Sanatana Dharma, or the Eternal Natural Way. We thus call ourselves "Dharmis", or followers of Dharma. We do not mix and match pure Vedic spirituality with any other religious traditions, modern "new age" innovations, or pop spirituality. To do so is to denigrate and reject Sanatana Dharma. We reject such empty and meaningless attempts as creating a form of 'spiritual' Radical Universalism. We exclusively identify with, and practice, Sanatana Dharma as our cherished path to self-realization and God-consciousness. It is only in single-minded fidelity to the path that we achieve the goal of the path.

167

Truth is not something that is haphazardly stumbled upon. Rather, it is acquired via the tried and tested means that have been employed by the greatest *yogis* and *rishis* since the beginning of time. We know truth by means of a) the instructing words and guidance of the enlightened teacher (*guru-vani*), b) the guidance of the revealed Vedic scriptures (*shastra-pramana*), and c) the use of our own reasoning faculties (*vichara*), philosophical discernment (*viveka*) and personal experience (*anubhava*). Sanatana Dharma is not a religion of blind faith, fanaticism, or wishful thinking. It is a religion of acquired spiritual and philosophical wisdom, coupled with direct personal experience of the transformative presence of God.

168

Wealth is eventually squandered. Beauty fades with time. Our possessions are all lost in the end. Power diminishes. Health dissipates. Material reality itself meets its final dissolution in the divine cosmic dance of Lord Shiva. But a love that is spiritually based...that is forever. Learn how to love the Divine first, then your family and people, and all sentient beings, and you will know the eternal.

169

Spiritual training (*sadhana*) consists of practicing the full classical Yoga system (*ashtanga*), permeated throughout with a consciousness of *bhakti* (devotion). *Bhakti*, or devotional consciousness, is understood to be both the highest means of liberation, as well as the ultimate goal of spiritual life and culture. Thus, *bhakti* is not merely the most effective means (*upaya*) for spiritual liberation; it is also the ultimate goal (*paramartha*) of life.

170

Aum Hari Aum. The seemingly opposed experiences of material happiness and material suffering are both ultimately illusory, and have no real or lasting affect on our inner consciousness. Our consciousness is eternal, beautiful and full of joy. It is who we truly are. It is the self-imposed illusion of ego and selfishness that has made us forget this fact. Yoga spirituality is designed to help us remember who and what we truly are. Aum Tat Sat.

171

As radically free individuals, each of us has the ability to honestly aspire toward the achievement of spiritual transformation and self-realization. Such spiritual attainment is to be achieved outside of the confines of sectarianism, intolerance, closed-minded fanaticism, and organizational denominationalism, and only in accordance with Dharma - the Natural Way of the Cosmos. Reject the artificial by freely embracing the Natural.

172

Human beings (*manushya*) are meant to live in a manner that best manifests for the entire world to witness the fact that we are spiritual beings temporarily inhabiting the material realm. In our innermost essence, we are beings who are free, eternal, beautiful, compassionate, wise and full of boundless joy. To live as spirit is to be human. To live as if we are matter is to be subhuman. Live as a truly human being, and be an example to the world of spiritual nobility.

173

We are meant to presence the Divine in our everyday lives, and to then humbly manifest infinite love, compassion, and wisdom toward all other beings.

174

Rather than reveling in exploitation of the Earth and our fellow living beings, we should grow in our dedication to serving others spiritually. Rather than rejoicing in our own greed, envy and anger, we should develop our natural spiritual capacity for giving, the celebration of life, and joy. Rather than live in fear and anxiety, we must embrace the full scope of our own boundless freedom. Reject the path of the demonic (*asurayana*) and embrace the path of the gods (*devayana*).

175

Truth is a reality that lies outside the confines of mere religious institutions and denominations. Rather, in the very best case scenario, religious institutions are meant to be mere temporal tools designed to direct the seeker to the Reality that lies beyond those very tools. True religion exists to surpass religion. To focus more on the institutions of spirituality rather than upon the purported goal of the institutions is similar to staring at the teacher's finger rather than gazing upon the eternal beauty that the teacher is pointing to.

176

A mindset of fanaticism represents a disturbed mental state in which the perceptions and cognitive reactions of the fanatic are unbalanced. Fanaticism is a psychological pathology. The opposite of fanaticism is balance. Balance leads to a psychological state of calm introspection, philosophical discernment, open-mindedness to reasonable propositions, and the desire to create a natural order rather than chaos in any given situation. One of the primary goals of the *yogi* is to achieve such balance.

177

Marxism is a demonic totalitarian system that is predicated upon the idea that the highest authority is derived from the lowest echelons of society, rather than from a Transcendent source. Marxist social theory has proven itself repeatedly to be thoroughly unworkable in any social-national construct. Dharma, on the other hand, teaches us that if we wish to create the very highest form of civilization, then we must derive our model from the most excellent and highest sources. Marxism seeks to make heaven into a hellish domain, while Dharma seeks to transform hell into a heavenly realm. Marxism is the very philosophical antithesis of Dharma - or Natural Law.

178

Raucous theological contention does not lead to Truth. Humble spiritual inquiry does. Thus we believe in dialogue, not debate; and in teaching, not preaching.

179

This illusory material world is an infinite ocean of individual *atmans* temporarily suffering from the effects of false ego. It is only by transcending your own illusory ego through Bhakti-yoga (union in devotional consciousness) that you can rise above that imprisoning ocean and be free of all illusion. Reject egotism, and know your true self (*atman*). Finally, surrender that pure self that you have discovered lovingly at the lotus-like feet of the Divine to know the sweetest bliss of true freedom. This is the ultimate conclusion (*siddhanta*) of Sanatana Dharma.

180

People possess freedom as an inherent attribute of their very soul (*atman*). Unfortunately, people also have the freedom to be in illusion. By extension, people have the freedom within their illusion to believe things that are the opposite of Reality. When they institutionalize such illusory beliefs, then we have man-made religion. Man-made religion is not synonymous with Sanatana Dharma - the Eternal Natural Way. Thus, all religions are not the same. All religions are not equal. As much as our sentiments (*bhavaka*) may wish to militate against this reality, reason (*anumana*) and discernment (*viveka*) tells us that all religions are not the same. To deny this fact is to take away people's innate freedom – including their freedom to choose to be in bondage to artificial, manmade religions.

181

Our tradition is called 'Vedic spirituality', or 'the Vedic tradition', or 'Vaidika Dharma' because the philosophy, practices and world-view upon which it is predicated is derived directly and exclusively from the Vedic scriptures. Of all the Vedic texts, the most accessible to us presently is the *Bhagavad Gita.* The *Bhagavad Gita* is the primary scripture for the Kali Yuga. The *Bhagavad Gita* was written to be an easier to understand summation of all the other Vedic scriptures. If you can understand the *Bhagavad Gita*, you can understand the *Vedas*. If you can understand the *Vedas*, you then possess the highest Truth.

182

The true *guru* has deep gravitas (*dhira*). He is an ocean of steadfastness, persistence, firmness, fortitude and strength. Being firmly situated in the center of calm that lies within, he establishes Dharma decisively for the benefit of the entire world.

183

The true *guru* serves as a clear window onto the spiritual realm. When we look upon such a liberated being, we see not merely a physical body alone. We see Dharma in motion.

184

Enlightened *yogis* inherently personify wisdom, compassion, moral goodness, dispassion, peace and spiritual love as the very essence of their being. Such *yogis* are, thus, the natural leaders of any society. We must look to the liberated *yogis* for guidance in not only spiritual matters, but in political, economic, cultural and social matters as well. Envision a world in which every president, prime minister and head of state were an enlightened *yogi*. Now work practically to manifest that spiritual vision into concrete reality. May the enlightened *yogis* guide us toward the creation of a true civilization. Evam bhavatu. May it be so.

185

For the enlightened *yogi*, the lover of God, neither time, nor place, have the same overpowering significance that they do for those still attached to the illusion of materialism. The liberated *yogi* is internally situated in a realm that is beyond both time and space. Such enlightened beings live always in the eternal. And Vaikuntha (the spiritual realm) is their only true home. Truth is their proper vehicle of language, and love is their reason for being.

186

The goal of Yoga is not to artificially renounce the world, but rather to engage in our duties in the world while spiritualizing our everyday lives. Yoga teaches us to be in the world, but not of the world.

187

In his own mind, the true *guru* does not see himself as anyone's master. Rather, he knows that he is everyone's servant. He is the servant of his students. He is the servant of his own *guru*. And he is the servant of God. Such healthy spiritual humility is what, in fact, makes him a perfect master.

188

Those who are suffering in the ignorance of illusion live as if they are situated in hell. They are in a hell of their own making. Those who are spiritually awake, however, know that hell, too, is nothing more than an insignificant illusion. Such awakened souls are always situated in a heavenly state.

189

From God's unlimited perspective, all of existence is a part of His divine *lila*, His joyous, playful pastimes. All of reality exists for the purpose of God's joy and pleasure alone. Thus, reality itself is a joyful realm. From our present limited viewpoint, however, we mistakenly view reality in accordance with our limited and distorted perspectival prism. We, as illusion-bound beings, tend to see both the universe, and God's relation to it, in a more limited functional dynamic because we necessarily view reality from within the context of our own seemingly separate interest. Upon cultivating our innate devotional consciousness (*bhakti*), however, then our perspectival awareness is transformed from seeing God in merely functional terms to then seeing that dynamic in purely spiritual terms; i.e., from God's unlimited perspectival vision. Only then, in a liberated state, do we as individual *atmans* have the ability to also understand the world and everything within it as being, indeed, God's perfect *lila* – God's perfect expressive joy. Nothing is outside of the scope of God or God's *lila*. Nothing exists outside of unlimited joy. There is only the temporary illusion that something exists outside of God and God's *lila*. To know and to experience this truth is the ultimate project of Yoga.

190

The illusory 'I' is a radically distinct imitation of the true 'I'. *Aham-kara*, or illusory ego, is an artificial sense of identity, and is thus dissolved upon liberation. However, *aham-pratyaya*, or I-cognition, remains eternally because it is an essential attribute of *atman*. *Aham-pratyaya* is our inherent, spiritual sense of 'I-ness', which is natural to *atman*. It is our inherent sense of self-awareness (*atma-bodhi*). We never lose our actual identity upon liberation, only our temporary false identity. We do not lose ourselves in liberation, as is the false claim of Advaitins and New Age demagogues. Rather, upon liberation, we find ourselves.

191

To ask questions of a spiritual master is a sign of intelligence. To even have some doubts at the very beginning of one's spiritual path is a healthy sign of philosophical cautiousness. To be decidedly offensive or combatant in one's supposed inquiry, however, is a sign of deep enviousness. Enviousness reveals to all that we were never serious in asking our questions to begin with. Cultivate sincerity and humility in your search for Truth, and you will know that Truth. The path of envy leads to the realm of darkness and ignorance alone.

192

When you surrender all that you are, as flower petals are offered at the lotus-like feet of the Divine, you then lose all fear. When you no longer fear, you discover an inner strength buried at the core of your being that is as calm as silence itself, but that has the power to stop even the elements of time and motion in their very trajectories. Do not hesitate to access that inner power quickly and fully if you wish to live a life of dignity and nobility even in the midst of this Kali Yuga (the current Age of Conflict). The systematic path of Yoga is the most effective way to overcome all fear, and to access that inner strength.

193

When approaching a true *guru*, one must never ask questions with arrogance, disrespect, impatience, or disregard for the importance and dignity of the Vedic process of learning. When one asks questions in such an offensive manner, the root psychological cause of such offensiveness is enviousness. The offensive person is not really interested in gaining a real answer to their question. They are merely upset that someone else is in the position to give them the answer. Thus the entire show of philosophical inquiry is itself nothing but an ego-driven charade on the part of the offensive person. Such an approach will never yield Truth, but only deeper levels of illusion. Inquire with humility and sincerity if you wish to approach Truth.

194

Truth is only known via a sincere, humble, open and eager desire to know the Truth. Philosophical arrogance closes the door to Truth. Loving devotion to that very Truth itself is the only way to open that door. Leave ego, envy and emotion outside the door when entering the domain of Truth.

195

Enlightened sages are mystics who precede and transcend all man-made denominations. Though religious bureaucracies are created in their names, they themselves belong to no human sect. Their true path is the Eternal Natural Way, which is above time, place and all material calculation. Thus, Gautama Buddha himself was never a Buddhist, but an enlightened follower of Dharma; Rishabha was never a Jaina, but was in actuality an enlightened follower of Dharma; Jesus himself was never a Christian, but was an enlightened follower of Dharma; Guru Nanak was never a Sikh, but was an enlightened follower of Dharma; Prabhupada himself was never a Hindu, but was a fully enlightened follower of Sanatana Dharma. All of these perfected sages were perfect Dharma Masters - pure devotees of the timeless Truth.

196

Beauty is not merely in the eye of the beholder. Beauty is not just what you see with your eyes or detect with your senses. Beauty in its purest form is an experience of a transcendent metaphysical phenomenon. It is an essential attribute and power (*shakti*) of the Divine. When you experience beauty in its deepest essence, you are experiencing God. At that point, you are not the beholder. Rather, beauty is beholding you.

197

Aum Hari Aum. Opinions about truth are subjective, but Truth itself is an objective reality. Opinions about truth are relative, but Truth itself is absolute. Opinions about truth are multiple, but Truth itself is one. Opinions lead to further illusion, but Truth leads to liberation. God is the highest Truth. Aum Tat Sat. That Absolute is Truth.

198

The nature of the truly authentic *guru* is such that when you are in the presence of such a true *guru*, your illusion is directly challenged by the truth of his words, by the lessons of his actions, and by the power of his very presence itself. To be in the presence of a true *guru* is to be in the presence of a roaring fire. He sheds his light and warmth upon you. But he must be approached with care and awareness. How you choose to react to the challenge that is the fire of the *guru* will reveal the quality of your own sincerity, humility, openness to guidance and yearning to know the Truth. Approach the presence of the *guru* wisely, and all will be revealed to you.

199

Almost every philosophical, theological and ideological contention in the world today ultimately stems from one basic question that most people cannot satisfactorily answer: 'What is your source of knowledge?' It is precisely due to having the lack of a credible answer to so fundamental an epistemological question that the world has degenerated into philosophical, ethical and spiritual relativism. At present, no one idea is allowed to be philosophically juxtaposed to another. We have been miseducated to believe that discernment is no longer a guide, and that truth is just a matter of subjective opinion. In a world in which all 'truths' are seen as equally legitimate, and in which sober and disciplined thinkers are bullied into silence, all so-called 'truths' are rendered equally untrue. The Sun of Truth has been purposefully hidden from our view behind an ominous veil of dark clouds for too long. Now that Sun of Truth is about to be released for the world to experience. Its light will illumine all. Satyam Eva Jayate.

200

The Vedic understanding of *guru* is that the *guru* does infinitely more than merely point one in the right direction. The *guru* personifies Truth in everything he or she thinks, says and does. As such, the *guru* provides a living example of what it means to live a life without illusion, is the conduit of grace that is necessary for final God-realization (*Brahma-vidya*), and has the ability to lead one directly to the highest reality. The *guru* empowers us in such a manner that we can be successful on the spiritual path. For these reasons, it is crucial that we have the indispensible grace of the *guru* if we are going to realize the purpose of the spiritual path.

201

By meditating directly upon that which is the highest source of all reality, we understand all of reality. By meditating directly upon that which is the original source of all that is good, we transform ourselves in such a way that there is nothing left within us but what is good. By meditating upon that which is not only consciousness itself, but which is the very source of all consciousness, we begin to understand our own consciousness. Meditate on the source. Meditate on the Supreme Godhead. In this way, you will perfect your life.

202

What one declares oneself to be is of less importance than what one actually practices. And what one practices externally is reflective of one's internal state of consciousness, one's inner motivations, one's inherent behavioral being (*svadharma*), and one's psycho-physiological nature (*varna*). Thus, one's declared philosophical stance should be a manifestation of one's inner state.

203

The true *guru* is fearless in the face of all atheistic opposition. He defends the dignity of Dharma at all costs to himself. He does not allow untruth to stand in his presence. The true *guru* does not know fear. In the presence of such a sage, darkness recedes, the demonic tremble, and the possibility of liberation from suffering becomes an open door to all.

204

Sanatana Dharma is a divine path the origins of which transcend both humanity and this world, but the full import of which can be understood by humanity in this world by the grace of *guru* and God. It is by the power of grace that the Transcendent can be known in a way that is imminent.

205

Being a purportedly spiritual person must never be used as an excuse for not also being an intelligent person. True spirituality cultivates and uses the necessary tool of intellect. True intelligence, on the other hand, means understanding the spiritual basis of reality. One must be both spiritual and intelligent for either pursuit to have ultimate meaning.

206

The Vedic way calls upon all intelligent human beings to become noble *(arya)* in their character and behavior. We become noble when we strive to achieve superlative excellence in every aspect of our lives. For the noble person, the ideal of striving for perfection in all things is never a cause for trepidation or excuses. Excellence is our very purpose in living. We live in order to exceed our present state. For the *arya* (the noble person), the attitude of either being or doing something that is 'good enough' can never be good enough. Strive always, and in every facet of your being, to be noble and excellent. *Praja arya jyotiragrah*. 'The *arya* are led by the divine light' (*Rig Veda*, 7.33.17).

207

It is Dharma that brings balance to our cosmos and to nature. We, too, are meant to live a life of balance by ordering our lives and environments in accordance with Dharma. Leading a balanced life, in which we peacefully reconcile the various positive qualities within ourselves, is an important element in achieving a state of excellence.

208

The Dharmi (follower of Sanatana Dharma) upholds all traditional Vedic values. These values are found universally among all civilized and noble peoples. Three of the most immediate of these Vedic values are: a) family, b) education, and c) a healthy work ethic. Family is the most important institution of any society. Education elevates the person in his or her knowledge, culture, tastes and character. Hard work creates disciple within the individual person and prosperity for society. These three values are the foundation of any healthy society and civilization.

209

The true *guru* is to be offered the greatest respect, loyalty, honor and regard imaginable. Our *guru* is the sacred portal between our life of illusion, and our eventual state of liberation and enlightenment. As such, our gratitude toward the *guru* knows no bounds. We do not use the *guru* and then throw him away when we think we are done with him. Indeed, when we mistakenly think that we are done with the *guru*, we have only shown that we are not even at the stage of a beginner on the spiritual path. We are forever linked with our divine guide on the path.

210

The true *guru* immediately stops his more foolish disciples from crossing from the boundary of healthy respect into the dark domain of offensiveness by claiming that the *guru* is God. There is no *guru* alive on the Earth today who can claim to be God, or a direct *avatara* of God. When a '*guru*' does not stop such behavior on the part of his mistaken followers - what to speak of actually encouraging it! - then that person has shown himself to be even more fallen than his very own disciples. He has revealed himself to the world to be not a *guru*, but simply a neophyte on the spiritual path. He is himself in need of surrender to, and instruction from, a true *guru*. No *guru* is literally God. No real *guru* would call himself God.

211

True love begins with the Source of all things. True love toward human beings, and toward all of creation, has its basis only in love of the Divine. It is only in loving God that we can claim to truly love God's creation. Otherwise, we are pouring water on the individual leaves of the tree without watering the all important root. God is the root of all reality.

212

Vedic spirituality pertains not merely to the past, but to the future of our planet. Vedic spirituality is going to form the very core of civilization in the very near future. The Dharma world-view and way of life is soon going to be the very center of politics, the center of economics, the center of science, and the center of all cultural expression. Dharma is going to become the center of our future civilization. It will be the present and future leaders of the International Sanatana Dharma Society who will bring this transformation about. Evam bhavatu - May it be so.

213

Only in the dark Abrahamic ideologies (Judaism, Christianity and Islam) is God portrayed as interacting with humanity through fear, guilt and hate. The god of Abrahamism is not the true and eternal God, the Source of all things. Sanatana Dharma, on the other hand, holds to a much higher conception of the Divine. In actuality, God only deals with us through mercy, through love, through compassion, and through grace. Sanatana Dharma teaches us that we are always surrounded by that grace; but we spend most of our lives unaware of that omni-present grace. Dharma is itself the grace of God in concretized form, as that grace becomes transformed in such a manner that we can have direct access to it within the material world. Though we desire to separate ourselves from God, God never separates Himself from us. It is in upholding Dharma that we know the grace of God.

214

We live in a world that is naturally rich in diversity. Diversity makes our world beautiful, interesting and meaningful. Diversity is itself a reflection of nature. Each individual human person, being a part of this natural diversity, is necessarily unique and different in comparison to every other human being. Men and women are uniquely different from one another. Cultures are uniquely different. Classes are uniquely different. Ethnicities and nationalities are uniquely different. Races are uniquely different. Religions are uniquely different. Languages are uniquely different. Indeed, no two leaves or blades of grass in all of creation are exactly the same. Dharma teaches us that such natural diversity needs to be honestly acknowledged and celebrated, and not artificially denied. Such diversity must never, on the other hand, be cynically manipulated as a cause for social and political conflict - as is always done by corrupt and malevolent politicians. Dharma fosters harmony within diversity. Dharma is, thus, quite literally the opposite of conflict. We are meant to bring about social harmony within the context of the natural diversity that we encounter in our world. It is with Dharma alone that we can sustain a meaningful and balanced unity in the face of natural diversity.

215

Hare Rama. We are currently experiencing the darkest period of the Kali Yuga that we have known up till now. For too long now have the enemies of Truth hidden the Sun of Dharma from our sight with their deception. We are once again going to see the Sun of Dharma arise in our lifetimes with a healing light that will illumine the entire world. Fear no darkness. The Sun rises. Hare Krishna.

216

The true sage does not know fear. Moreover, he protects all others from the greatest of fears. When the true sage is present, all other beings run to that person as an invincible shelter in the face of danger. Seek always the banner of such a sage, and let him lead you to victory over darkness. Aum Sri Gurubhyo Namaha.

217

The only truly authoritative source for transcendental knowledge is a source that is infinitely higher than we ourselves have the capacity to duplicate. God is that source; and that transcendental knowledge is revealed to humanity through the *Vedas* and the sacred words of the *guru*.

218

The most immediate and affective means of knowing the Perfect is to go to the Perfect for perfect knowledge. The Perfect reveals His perfect nature in the Vedic scriptures. Thus, the Vedic scriptures are themselves perfect by direct extension. Always go to the source of all true knowledge and wisdom. Always go to the Perfect. God, as revealed in the Vedic scriptures, is that Perfect.

219

All beings seek the highest good for themselves, whether that good is in the form of beauty, health, love, wealth, bliss, or any other goal. These are all merely subordinate derivatives, however, of which God is the ultimate source. God is that being who is in possession of an infinite number of auspicious attributes that are expressed to an infinite degree of depth. God is the source of all that is auspicious, all that is good, all that is true, all that is beautiful, and all that is of ultimate value in reality. Know that source, who is God, and you will know all things in their perfect and most fulfilling form.

220

Do we wish to merely meditate upon that which is the third or fourth or tenth highest? If our meditation practice is to have any honest meaning, then we should commit ourselves to meditate only upon that which is truly the very highest of all realities. It is by meditating directly upon that which is the highest source of all reality that we understand reality. Meditate always on the highest. Meditate always on God, on Bhagavan Sri Krishna. To meditate upon anything less than our highest source is simply to use the very meditative practice itself as a means to cheat ourselves. Hari Aum Tat Sat.

221

We must never be afraid to give of ourselves in service to God. When we give even the smallest item in devotion to God, God then gives infinitely to us. The Infinite necessarily reciprocates with the finite to an infinite degree. God always gives us more than we deserve.

222

Not all compassion is equal or the same. There is materialistic compassion, and there is spiritual compassion. The former is a lesser compassion, while the latter is a greater compassion. Even an *asura* (demonic person), after all, can seemingly exhibit a lesser 'compassion'. But the cynically motivated compassion of the *asura* is based upon the bodily conception alone. It is done merely for show. When we give out of materialistic compassion in the bodily concept of life, such giving is an external act alone. Such lesser compassion only produces more *karma*. It is only when we understand the temporality of the body, and the fact that we are all eternal souls, that we can then show true compassion, which is spiritual in nature. This greater compassion is based upon self-realization, upon wisdom, and upon spiritual insight. The greatest compassion of all is to help people spiritually, to help people realize their true self. This is the highest compassion that we can express. Such spiritual compassion produces liberation upon the performer, and even potentially upon the recipient.

223

Our spiritual dilemma is that we are currently suffering from a form of spiritual amnesia. We have forgotten who and what we really are. The greatest suffering that we can have is to not know ourselves. The greatest joy is to awaken to our true identity. Awake and arise to your true self. Do not merely accept the dreamlike reality that you have settled into.

224

Aum Shanti. Meditation is focused awareness upon one object. When you are meditating properly, nothing exists for you except for that upon which you are meditating. Proper meditation means having perfect focus. Make the Divine your object of perfect meditational focus. Such a perfect meditational state is Brahma-vidya, God-consciousness. Aum Namo Narayanaya.

225

The fact that every individual thinks that they have the truth does not, in itself, negate the fact that there is an objective truth to be known. Truth does not depend upon us or upon our opinions of it for its validity. We, on the contrary, depend upon Truth. Do not use the existence of a multiplicity of flawed opinions as a convenient excuse to not look for that Truth. If you seek Truth with sincerity, humility, openness, and eagerness, that Truth will be revealed to you – despite the dark jungle of flawed opinion that now temporarily obstructs your vision.

226

You know that you have finally encountered the highest Truth when your questions are at last fully satisfied. When your heart is overflowing with joy, your mind is at peace, and you now recognize that the entirety of reality is your very best friend, you have then achieved the highest Truth. At this point, the search has come to an end. You are spiritually fulfilled.

227

Spirituality is a celebration of consciousness, of who we are as eternal spirit. Spirituality is life. When we negate life, we deny consciousness. When we deny consciousness, we deny ourselves as spiritual beings. The opposite of life is death. Having denied humanity a meaningful life of the spirit, the culture of the 20th and 21st centuries has been a culture of death, a celebration of death. Sanatana Dharma is a culture of spirituality, of consciousness and of life. Let us now begin to celebrate life once again.

228

Dharma and *adharma* (anti-Dharma) are opposite paths. That which elevates us, makes us healthier and more whole either spiritually, intellectually, culturally, or in any other way that we can think of, that is Dharma. Anything that denigrates us, makes us less healthy, or less whole in any manner is *adharma*, the opposite of Dharma. Dharma is life. Adharma is death. Follow always the path of Dharma if you wish to elevate your existence.

229

Any notion of equality that is artificially imposed via legislation, social engineering, or political ideology is based upon a destructive myth. The diversity inherent in Nature bears testimony to this fact. Every individual material body, mind and personality is different from every other. Some living beings are stronger, some are more beautiful, some are bigger in size, some have more character, and some are healthier. Some intellects are greater, some lesser. There is no equality between any two individual material bodies, minds or personalities. But there is qualitative approximation on the higher level of spirit. The true basis of equality lies in the recognition that we are not merely these diverse bodies, composed of insentient matter, but that we are the pure, eternal soul lying within. It is only in accepting spiritual equality, and rejecting artificially imposed material equality, that justice is assured.

230

One of the most philosophically vacuous slogans of the New Age movement is the stated dogma that '*we are all one*'. While such a pronouncement may be appealing to the innocent public's sentiment, this dogma is deceivingly insufficient to describe the true spiritual connection held between all living beings. All living beings share in the same ontological nature spiritually. We all have Sriman Narayana as our divine Source. Consequently, we all share in the same qualitative essence. All living beings are consciousness. It is in this strictly ontological sense alone that one can state that '*we are all one*' (*abheda*). But we are all also eternally diverse individuals. It is in this strictly elementary indentitarian sense that we are different (*bheda*). In our spiritual essence (*svarupa*), we are all naturally variegated, both from each other and from the Absolute. Thus, we are all one, and simultaneously all different. Given this deeper understanding of 'oneness', we must not use the often misunderstood concept of oneness as yet one more excuse to lose ourselves in the illusion of false identity. We are both one, and beautifully different at the same time. Spiritual reality consists of a healthy and natural unity in diversity.

231

Spiritual information is only as reliable as is the person who is providing the information.

232

Taxation is theft. Government institutions at all levels of society are steeped in unbridled corruption, bureaucracy and tyranny in direct proportion to how much money they confiscate from their citizens' hard-earned wages. It is for this reason that taxation must be reduced to the very lowest levels necessary for the minimal functioning of government. Wealth belongs exclusively in the hands of those who create wealth. As its creators, only private citizens have the wisdom and prudence to use and distribute their money efficiently. It is private citizens who create everything of value, and not the state.

233

God is the source of all true beauty. Whenever we encounter overpowering instances of beauty in our lives, whether in nature, art or other living beings, we are encountering aesthetic vortices that serve as windows to the presence of God. Beauty is thus a vivid path for knowing the Divine. Cultivate beauty in yourself, in your surroundings and in society, and you will directly presence the living beauty of the Divine.

234

The Vedic path is primarily a spiritual warrior culture - tempered by a sacred duty of upholding Dharma. Vedic spirituality is a culture that encourages strength, courage, discernment, nobility, excellence, discipline, self-sacrifice for the highest ideal, and steadfastness in the face of injustice. Sanatana Dharma is not a path for the weak-hearted. It is the way of the Dharma warrior. It is the path of heroes.

235

We are subjective beings living in an objective reality. Our *atman* is subjective. It is non-different from our essential personality. It is the seat of our personal perspectives, tastes, experiences and idiosyncrasies. Brahman (God), on the other hand, is the objective reality in which our subjective *atman* operates. The objective reality of Brahman is absolute, unalterable, stable and eternal. It is when we mistake our own subjective perspective for the whole reality that we are in illusion. It is only when the subjective (*atman*) and the objective (Brahman) are aligned in a healthy and balanced way that we are living in accordance with perfect Dharma.

236

However small or powerless you may sometimes think you are in the face of malevolent forces, you need to always remember that, in actuality, you have been provided with infinite power within to face any challenge. You are a spark of the Divine. You are a beloved child of God. There is nothing more empowering than being a child of God. You are not powerless. You are not alone. Do not ever fear any darkness.

237

The fundamental claim of Radical Universalism is that a) all of the varying, individual religious traditions, sects, denominations and paths that presently exist, in addition to all those that have ever existed historically, all share the exact same ultimate salvific goal, and that b) all theological systems are equally valid philosophically, despite the fact that their individual claims on truth are irreconcilably contradictory when these systems are analytically juxtaposed. In simpler terms, Radical Universalism makes the philosophically untenable claim that '*all religions are the same*'. Sanatana Dharma teaches us that all religions and world-views are not exactly the same. To artificially render all religions exactly equal is actually to show equal disrespect to the internal qualities of all religions. It is only through philosophical discernment and intellectual honesty that we can fully understand this truth.

238

The greater cosmos is a well-ordered and integrated whole. It is a self-contained *mandala* of cosmic proportions. Our sustenance in the form of food comes to us from the Earth. The Earth, in turn, grows food as a result of the blessing of rain. Rain is brought forth as a result of prayer, ceremony and sacrifice to the gods, who are the providers of rain. When the gods are pleased us, they then provide all the bountiful blessings of nature. The knowledge of such ceremonies is revealed to the sages directly from God. The sages nourish their bodies and minds from the food that the Earth provides. Such is the harmoniously interdependent nature of Dharma. Aum Tat Sat.

239

Aham Brahmasmi. The basic foundation of all meaningful philosophy is the proper understanding of the true nature of the soul. It was with this understanding that Socrates advised the seeker of truth to "Know thyself". If one does not even know one's own self, then how can one truthfully claim to possess any knowledge of anything at all? He who wishes to know anything at all must first know the knower. Tat Tvam Asi.

240

An unethical person cannot also claim to be a spiritual person. Unless you have a solid ethical foundation grounding your life, you will not be adequately equipped to engage in the search for wisdom. This is why the very beginning of spiritual life consists of building character, nobility, self-discipline, honesty and a very strong ethical life. Indeed, a so-called spiritual search without an ethical foundation only leads to further illusion, as well as disrespect and abuse of the very spiritual path one claims to follow. Without an ethical foundation, spiritual life has not yet even begun.

241

The power of knowledge is analogous to medicine. Not all knowledge is provided in the same way in direct relation to the individual who is acquiring the knowledge. Like medicine, knowledge must be taken in the correct dose, in the most effective manner, at the proper time, and from the right source. Otherwise, it may end up doing more harm than good. The true *guru* is the expert physician who will proscribe our spiritual medicine accordingly.

242

Ritual and ceremonial worship (*puja*) are a central function in all ancient forms of spirituality. There is no authentic spiritual tradition that is completely devoid of all ritual and ceremonial practice. Ritual is as important a spiritual discipline as are the practices of Yoga and meditation. Indeed, proper ritual is non-different from Yoga and meditation. Ritual can, however, be performed in a way that is empty of meaning and power if it is practiced without proper intention. It is only when the proper devotional intention is absent that ritual practice becomes empty 'ritualism'. The actual practice of spiritual rituals is meant to be performed as a conscious meditation. One must be in a deep state of devotional awareness, and focused upon the ultimate meaning and goal of the ritual if the ritual practice is to have a transformative effect upon the practitioner. Practiced in this way, ritual is a crucial tool in spiritual life that also helps to bring a deep sense of order and discipline in one's daily life.

243

The intelligent spiritual seeker must explore reality vertically, and not merely horizontally. He must fix his philosophical gaze upward toward transcendence in his yearning for Truth, and not just across the spectrum of finite things and flawed opinions. Truth comes from that which is ontologically above.

244

Mere intellectual curiosity, without the benefit of a sincere yearning to surrender to Truth, is not sufficient for realizing Truth. Seek Truth from above, and not merely from your own flawed intellect or the flawed opinions of others.

245

Jean Jacque Rousseau's famous statement that 'man was born free, and everywhere he is in chains' somewhat approximates a true statement. Unfortunately, Rousseau viewed man's dilemma solely from the materialist viewpoint as being primarily a social, political and economic crisis. Man's bondage is in actuality primarily a spiritual dilemma, and man's freedom can only be meaningfully addressed in spiritual terms. His chains consist of a self-imposed ignorance and egotism of his own, freely chosen creation. His freedom is likewise only secured by freely embracing wisdom and surrender to the Divine. Man is inherently free, and has chosen to create his own chains of illusion. May he now choose to re-embrace his inherent freedom.

246

The greatest enemy of the philosopher is intellectual arrogance. His greatest ally is humility.

247

In our attempts to share the truth of Dharma with others, we must never offend or disrespect them. Aggressive methods of outreach create unnecessarily adversarial situations, which only serve to close permanently otherwise potentially open minds. We must create understanding, not discord; dialogue, not confrontation; sympathy, not intolerance. We believe in teaching, not preaching. But teach we must.

248

To say that the presence of water is a universal constant that can be found everywhere in our world is not the equivalent of claiming that everything that exists in our world is water. Water is everywhere; but not everything is justifiably termed water. In the same way, to say that Dharma is a universal concept is not the equivalent of claiming that all religions, philosophies and ideologies are of the nature of Dharma. Dharma is everywhere; but not everyone embraces Dharma. While Dharma is meant for everyone, not everyone is necessarily ready for Dharma. Thus, all religions, philosophies and world-views are not the same.

249

Spiritual attainment is a two-stage progression through a) self-realization, followed by b) God-consciousness. The first is *atman* (self) realization. The second is Paramatman (Highest Self) realization. Self-realization represents the beginning stage of full enlightenment. In order to have perfect knowledge of God, who is the greatest object of all knowledge, first you have to know the knower. You must first know who is the knower before you can know that which is the highest transcendent reality. Once we know our true self (*atman*), only then we can hope to know He who is the very source of that essential self.

250

Aum Hari Aum. You are soul. You are consciousness. You are *atman.* Freedom is an innate attribute of your *atman.* Therefore, you are inherently free. There is an infinite expanse that is lying before you to freely explore. The whole of that infinite expanse is the realm of the Supreme Absolute. Enter that infinite expanse with all your enthusiasm and devotion. Through such devotion toward the Supreme Absolute, you will know happiness. You will know all. This is the proper use of your innate freedom. Aum Tat Sat.

251

Attempting to practice the path of Yoga without having the Divine in the center of one's practice is to defeat the actual purpose of Yoga. It is similar to trying to be a professional chef without ever using actual food in the process of cooking, or claiming to be a lover of deep nature while never having ventured out of your 14th floor Manhattan apartment. Such a path of supposed 'Yoga' is form only, but with no meaningful substance. It is empty. The true sweetness of the Yoga path is experienced in surrendering to the bliss of devotional consciousness (*bhakti*) toward the Divine. Yoga means 'union'. Experience your innate union with the Divine through authentic Yoga practice. Only then will your Yoga practice be brought to life.

252

There is no practice as empowering and life changing as meditation. It is wonderful that an increasing number of Westerners are turning to meditation - even if only to relieve to some degree the stress and existential angst caused by the secular materialism of post-modernity. Most, however, seem to turn to the ancient science of meditation as nothing more than a stress-relief exercise. While meditation does relief stress and anxiety, this is only a secondary benefit of meditation practice. The primary reason why we should meditate is to know ourselves and to know God. It is important that meditation never be artificially divorced from it ancient roots as a spiritual practice designed to bring about self-realization and God-consciousness. Meditation is not a pop, New Age fad. It is the very heart of Yoga and Vedic spirituality. Meditation is the path to enlightenment.

253

Our world is currently in the midst of many crises. It is up to each of us to do what is necessary to restore sanity to the world. If we truly want to help bring about substantial change in the social-political realm today, then we must only support and vote for those candidates for political office who verbally denounce the establishment of a new, totalitarian world order and who support decentralization of all authority to the most local levels. In how we acquire information, how we think, how we communicate, how we entertain ourselves, how we shop, how we affect our world, how we vote, and in how we live, we must always use the wisdom gifted to us as the mature fruit of Yoga and meditation.

254

American New Age spirituality relates to authentic spirituality in the same way that McDonald's relates to healthy organic food, the way elevator music relates to aesthetically transcendent cultural expressions, and the way 'reality TV' relates to actual reality. New Age spirituality has no connection to authentic spirituality at all. If you wish to have a meaningful spiritual experience and a reliable understanding of Truth, then seek an ancient and authentic spiritual tradition and follow it with fidelity, patience, humility and dedication. Serve the tradition rather than expecting the tradition to serve you. There is no Truth in modern American spiritual consumerism.

255

Kirtana (Vedic devotional music) is not an entertainment experience. Neither is it designed to be merely a vehicle to release pent up emotion or sentimentality. *Kirtana* is a worship experience. It is in *kirtana* that our hearts reach out in yearning devotion toward God.

256

Knowing the balanced distinction between the spiritual and the practical is crucial if we are going to practice compassion in any meaningful way. All too many people think that what it means to forgive someone is that we release them from their own responsibilities, liabilities and duty to do the right thing. That is not the case. Part of the forgiveness process is insisting that the person whom we are forgiving must now change his ways and do the right thing. We can and must forgive, while also always pursuing justice as well. Injustice is the opposite of Dharma. True forgiveness can never lead to injustice, but only to justice.

257

Through our ancestral heritage, we are all part of an historic continuum stretching back to the very beginning of time. We must never reject the past significance our family, our ancestors, and our people. Those who are no longer living in physical form have not ceased to be valuable members of our present community. Though they have gone on to the realm of the ancestors, they are still an integral part of our family. They still care for us and guide us in myriad unseen ways. Find comfort, strength and inspiration from your ancestral heritage. It is only in honoring the sanctity of our ancient spiritual heritage that we will secure a future that has true meaning and beauty.

258

Dark beings and evil people derive a perverse pleasure in manipulating and harming good people. Such entities may seem at first sight to be powerful. That is only because their very existence is based upon illusion, upon a lie. Like the parasitic entities they truly are, such insignificant beings feed upon our very fear itself. The moment they realize, however, that we have zero reason to fear them, they run away screeching as fast as their tiny feet can take them. They are, and always were, nothing more than paper tigers. We can poke our finger right through them if we so desire. Even the seemingly smallest of good people can render evil beings into complete nonexistence - effortlessly - because such evil little people never had any real existence to them to begin with. Know that the strength and the power is with you. It always was.

259

To see Krishna in all things, at all times, everywhere is the perfection of spiritual vision.

260

Like a fire without its brilliance; like a forest devoid of its trees; like a lion that is toothless; a *yogi* without virtue is a *yogi* who is devoid of his inherent power and spiritual strength. It is for this reason that Patanjali lists the ethical virtues of *yama* and *niyama* first and foremost in his *ashtanga* (eight-limbed) system of Yoga.

261

What is a true *guru*? A true *guru* would rather live a life of poverty and obscurity before veering even one iota from Truth. A fake *guru*, on the other hand, will eagerly veer light-years away from Truth if it means that he will achieve wealth and fame. Only a true *guru* can lead you onto the sure path to enlightenment.

262

To be a *yogi* is to live your life as a celebration of authenticity, of meaning, and of sincere dedication to Truth. The path of Yoga demands nothing less of you.

263

God gives, not merely in accordance with what we have earned, but with what we deserve. What we have earned is a reflection of our external skill, talent and abilities. But what we deserve is a reflection of our inner being. The world responds to externals. God responds to the internal person.

264

Dharma is manifest in the world around us in the form of the natural diversity that we witness in all things. Radical Egalitarianism, the artificial suppression of all inherent differences, leads to the eradication of such natural diversity. Radical Egalitarianism is, thus, the opposite of Dharma. It is the opposite of the natural. To celebrate true natural diversity, we must reject Radical Egalitarianism and take refuge in Dharma.

265

Followers of Sanatana Dharma believe in teaching, not preaching. But we do believe in teaching. When we see others around us who are in pain and suffering, we must lovingly share the teachings of Vedic philosophy with them out of great compassion and caring. It is in helping all sentient beings to grow spiritually that we are truly expressing the greatest love. To share Dharma with others is truly to be compassionate.

266

Jesus was not a follower of Judaism, Christianity or Islam. Jesus was a Dharma Master. In order to fully understand and practice the teachings of Jesus in a truly pure and authentic manner, it will be necessary for contemporary followers of Jesus to completely reject all traces of Abrahamism that have corrupted the original teachings of Jesus for the last two millennia. Such a re-embrace of Jesus' original message entails a thorough rejection of the Old Testament and the artificial god of the Old Testament, who was not the God of Jesus. It also requires the rejection of the fallacies of Paul recorded in the New Testament. Reestablishing the original message of Jesus means reintroducing the concepts of reincarnation, vegetarianism, meditation, mysticism and eternal wisdom (Gnosis) that Jesus himself followed and taught. It also means offering the greatest respect toward women, as Jesus himself displayed for us through his love of Mary Magdalene, his closest disciple. Only upon such an exorcism of the poisons of Abrahamism will 'Christians' truly understand the authentic teachings of Christ.

267

At this important transitional juncture in the Kali Yuga, conventional political movements are doomed to failure from the start. They are all ultimately ineffective. This is due either to faulty leadership within such movements, infiltration by various malevolent provocateurs with decades of experience in creating discord in such transformative movements, or more often than not a combination of both of the above. The only way to radically change our culture today is through an empowered spiritual movement designed to help transform people at the very core of their consciousness. Change a person's inner reality, and you will ensure sweeping social transformation. Such a movement can only be led by someone who is highly qualified to lead. Such a spiritual movement is our only hope for fundamental and positive societal transformation. *The Dharma Manifesto* is the exact blueprint for such a movement. It will empower its readers to change the very face of our present world!

268

For fundamentalist Christians, Jesus is someone to simply worship from afar in fear and reverence. For unsophisticated New Age zealots, Jesus is a crystal gazing Space Brother. In actuality, Jesus is our *guru* beckoning us to eventually become as he is. If you wish to understand Jesus, be as Jesus is.

269

Tragically, the qualifications for what is considered to be a 'spiritual teacher' today have now degenerated beyond recognition. There are presently thousands of people in America alone (and this certainly can be applied to Europe and India as well) who suffer from what I have termed 'Premature Guru Syndrome'. These are individuals who tend to be relatively new to the path, and who have very few actual qualifications, or knowledge, or moral integrity to even be considered beginners on the spiritual path, what to speak of 'Masters'. Despite not being qualified, however, many of these dishonest individuals have nonetheless deluded themselves into thinking that they are now *'gurus'* (in some cases, even *'avataras'*!). Such frauds have both harmed the reputation of the Vedic tradition itself, as well as abused an untold number of innocent spiritual seekers in a myriad of terrible ways. I have spoken out against such Premature Guru Syndrome for many decades now, often at great personal expense, and much concerted retaliation against my teaching mission. I hope an increasing number of respected Vedic leaders will now begin to speak out publicly about such sociopathic spiritual abusers. It is up to all followers of Vedic spirituality to foster the courage and integrity necessary to speak the truth in order to preserve the honor of our great Sanatana Dharma tradition. Aum Shanti.

270

When each distinct People honor their own ancestors, it leads to the empowering of that specific ethnic group in a manner that solidifies their community both spiritually and temporally. Each and every ethnic group should be encouraged to honor and derive inspiration from the divinities of their own folk traditions. This is a crucial spiritual linkage with the past that the Abrahamic onslaught always sought to destroy at its roots. Now, thankfully, each distinct People is reclaiming their own spiritual folk-roots again. Honor your ancestors, and you will deepen your knowledge of yourself. Know your past, and you will be equipped to secure your future.

271

The truly enlightened spiritual teachers of the past had loyalty to Dharma rather than to any artificially concocted religious sects. The great sages Rishabhadeva, Gautama Buddha, Jesus, and Guru Nanak, specifically, were all master *yogis* and faithful followers of Sanatana Dharma. None of these liberated *gurus* shared the Truth with their disciples with the intention that separate and distinct sects would eventually be founded in their names. None of these sages concocted new sects. Their followers did in their sacred names. If we can filter out all of the sectarian-derived dogmas that were artificially developed during the centuries after these original Dharma Masters left our world, the pure essence that remains is Sanatana Dharma, the Eternal Natural Way.

272

The masses derive their misperceived impression of reality from an attenuated combination of flawed opinion, the subtle propaganda of the entertainment/media complex, the most recent fads masquerading as profound ideas, and an educational system more geared toward producing conformity in its students than cultivating inherent reasoning skills. Such deficient sources only further the illusion of the common person. Truth, on the other hand, is not derived from such spiritually crippling sources. The *yogi* derives his embrace of true Reality from a humble study of the Vedic scriptures, the words of a genuine and qualified *guru*, from the power of wisdom and reason, and from his own inner realization derived directly from meditation, prayer and spiritual practice (*sadhana*). In this way, the *yogi* enters into the stream of eternal Truth, which does not change in accordance with the latest fashion. Truth is to be known through the path of the *yogi*. Seek the path of the *yogi* if you wish to free your mind.

273

One of the most often parroted phrases that we hear echoed today by shallow New Age zealots is the philosophically empty term 'judgmental'. We are warned by these militant relativists that the greatest of all unforgivable sins is to be 'judgmental'. The New Age term 'judgmental', however, is not a concept that can be acknowledged as having any meaningful intellectual content. To call someone 'judgmental' is, of course, in itself 'judgmental', thus rendering the very term itself self-contradictory and meaningless. More important than the obvious contradictory absurdity of the New Age wrath against being 'judgmental' is the fact that rendering rational judgments is an inherently natural component of the faculty of human intellect. As human beings, we are designed to use our discernment, discrimination, reason, and logic in order to judge the nature, efficacy and ethical content of any given situation, proposition, or course of action. To not judge is be without a mind! To not be 'judgmental' is to not be human. This said, some persons are clearly in more of a position to judge, while some others are very clearly not in such a position. Those who are in such a position are very few. Such persons are the wise sages, enlightened *yogis* and liberated *rishis* whose words of judgment we should respect, honor and follow with sincerity.

274

Truth descends from above, in a vertical fashion, from the heavenly realm coming down to the earthly plane, and not from the level of horizontal imperfection. Truth comes from God, not from Man. Do not seek Truth in the flawed and self-motivated opinions of imperfect humans beings. Seek Truth in the Transcendent if you wish to have perfect knowledge.

275

We are currently residing in the Kali Yuga, the most decadent and materialistic of ages. The negative influence of this age makes all spiritual pursuit much more challenging than it would have been in previous ages. The personal struggle necessary to make meaningful spiritual progress today is thus immense. The best way to counteract the ill effects of the Kali Yuga is to live as if we are already denizens of the Satya Yuga (Golden Age). This means living with honor, nobility, excellence and spirituality as the core center of our beings. We must behave in such a manner that we are worthy of a Golden Age. As a result, the Golden Age will reward us with its presence, both in our individual lives and in our immediate society. The time of riding the tiger is soon to be behind us. We will now bring the tiger into submission.

276

We have been systematically brainwashed to believe that the traditional wisdom of the historic past is an oppressive enemy to be overcome and rejected. The opposite is actually the case. Our ancestors are among our greatest teachers and benefactors. Our past heritage is a deep treasure trove of indispensible knowledge, beauty, culture and spiritual nourishment from which we can learn and grow. The past is an integral component of our present community. Learn from the eternal wisdom of the ancient sages and the sacred scriptures that they left for us, as well as of the example of your own ancestors, and you will know wisdom, connection and contentment.

277

It is tragic how many otherwise seemingly idealistic people believe that the end justifies the means in forwarding their cause. The end never justifies the means - regardless of what the goal is claimed to be. The ethical content of the means must always be analyzed on its own terms. If the means is unethical, it is to be rejected – regardless of what the purported end goal may be. To disregard ethical conduct and virtue is to morally demean both the person and the very goal itself, and to render both devoid of God's grace, and thus ultimate meaning. Evil only begets the very opposite of Dharma. Only good begets the good. Only Dharma begets Dharma.

278

Dharma social-political activists call themselves Dharma Nationalists, not because they are nationalists in any mere xenophobic or territorial sense of the term. Their ideology transcends any simplistic pride of place or geographical chauvinism. Rather, Dharma activists refer to themselves as Dharma Nationalists because their ultimate goal is to bring about the eventual establishment of multiple nation-states that govern their respective peoples in accordance with the eternal principles of Dharma, or Natural Law. A Dharma Nation is not a nation founded upon a place, but upon a principle. Wherever Dharma is being followed by any given society, that place is our nation. Our aspiration is nothing less than manifesting the eternal Dharma Nation. Dharma Rashtra Jayate.

279

In direct proportion to how elevated one ascends in one's understanding of Truth (*satya*), the smaller one's circle of associates naturally becomes. While the most general of truths are easily accepted by the majority of people with little difficulty or resistance, the more particularized, esoteric and breathtaking the degree of Truth is, the fewer are the number of people fully capable of appreciating it. The greatest truths are known only by the very few. Thus, Patanjali terms the state of liberation *kevalam*, or distinctiveness. The rarest of those very few are the *sad-gurus*, the true spiritual masters. It is these liberated beings especially whom we must approach in our pursuit of the most elevated Truth.

280

Those who understand the true nature of spirituality gauge spiritual growth not merely in terms of numerical advancement or quantitative progression. Rather, a person's spiritual advancement is understood in terms of the qualitative depth of his experience and attainment. The notion of quantity applies primarily to the material world, and not to the spiritual realm. In spiritual reality, quantity exists merely as the servant of quality.

281

The majority of Yoga centers today are teaching only the outer form of Yoga, and neglecting the essential spiritual dimension of the path. Thus, in many cases there is little distinction between venues in which the sacred tradition of Yoga is taught and dance studios. We must now transform all current-day Yoga 'studios' into Yoga Temples. Such temples of Yoga must be oases of spiritual refuge, divine fellowship (*satsangha*), and shelters in which people may experience much needed relief from the sufferings of this world. Yoga is not merely one more means of working up an aerobic sweat! Yoga is our path for realizing the Divine. It is only if we celebrate the spiritual essence of our path with the respectful dignity that it deserves that we will understand the very heart of Yoga. Only then can we call ourselves *yogis*.

282

Many of the most important philosophical propositions of the Vedic scriptures have been a cause of bewildered trepidation for the majority of modern theologians, philosophers, academicians and scientists. This has been the case because they have attempted to grasp the Vedic truth via mere discursive thought rather than through inner realization. Consequently, most of the writings of such academicians on the topic of Vedic spirituality has been severely lacking in insight. It is only by becoming like the *rishis* that we can fully understand the profound words of the *rishis* that are contained in the Vedic scriptures. All else is mere academic fluff.

283

The ultimate revolutionary undertaking of the twenty-first century will be the thorough dismantling of materialism itself. Sanatana Dharma Vijayate.

284

It is easy to love others when they shower love and affection upon us. What it means to be a good person is that you will often chose to love others despite sometimes not being loved in return. That is selfless love.

285

The spiritual practitioner and the Dharma warrior share in the same inner qualities and challenges. Both the spiritual practitioner and the Dharma warrior must strive to cultivate a character that is honorable. What it means to be honorable is to have honesty, integrity and authenticity in everything that we do.

286

The follower of Sanatana Dharma seeks the greatest degree of excellence in everything that he thinks, says and does. He seeks quality and distinction in both himself and everything he creates.

287

It is the worst of myths that Vedic spirituality encourages people to be passive and weak. The very opposite is the case. The path of Sanatana Dharma, when it is properly understood, teaches us to be courageous, strong and noble. Sanatana Dharma is the path of lions.

288

There is no force in existence that can defeat Sanatana Dharma. Neither can anything ever truly defeat the noble Dharma Warrior. Even if the Dharma Warrior seems to die in the defense of Truth, his glory lives on forever. Never hesitate to be an invincible and courageous Dharma Warrior!

289

We live in a dense forest of opinions. Everyone has an opinion. Truth, however, is not subject to anyone's opinion. Truth is not to be found in opinion. It is to be found in God. Subjective opinion is only shadow. But God is the Sun. Look to God and to God's representative if you desire to know Truth.

290

In our love of God, the impossible happens. Every door is opened. Our freedom becomes boundless. Our joy knows no end. There are no limits ever placed upon our reciprocal loving relationship with the Divine. It is in loving God that we know the Infinite fully.

291

The so-called Ancient Aliens theory has presented the opposite of what is the real case. It has mistaken the phenomenon of mankind's encounters with extraterrestrial beings in the reverse of the true scenario. It is not that the gods and demons of the ancient world were all nothing more than so-called aliens. Rather, many of today's encounters with supposed aliens are, in actuality, modern manifestations of very real gods and demons. Gods and demons are not relegated to a distant and superstitious past. On the contrary, they are at the very least as real as we are, if not more so. Extraterrestrials are not the 'space scientists' of popular science fiction. They are actually the metaphysical beings that the world's many spiritual traditions, sacred scriptures and wise sages have spoken of. Rather than 'ancient aliens', people today are directly encountering modern gods and demons.

292

Our consciousness becomes colored by that which we bring into our consciousness. It is for this reason that the *yogi* strives for complete control over the senses. Mastery of the senses is the beginning of the spiritual path. We must always keep all negative and dark influences out of our consciousness, and only allow the good and the spiritual to come into our consciousness. In this way, we will be elevated rather than denigrated. We will be free rather than bound.

293

To achieve self-realization is the first task of the spiritual seeker. Even more satisfying than knowing my true self (*atman*), however, is to then know that which is the very Source of my true self. That source is Paramatman, or the Supreme Self – God. This is the higher pursuit because, if I know that Source, then I will know all things, including my own true self.

294

Vegetarianism is neither a leftwing, nor a rightwing concern. Vegetarian is about compassion and respect for life. Protecting the natural environment is neither a leftwing, nor a rightwing concern. Protecting nature is about securing the health and wellbeing of our families and of our Mother, the Earth. Yoga and Meditation are neither leftwing, nor rightwing concerns. Yoga spirituality is about spiritually transforming our essential being and directly experiencing God. The Vedic path transcends all contemporary ideological categories. The goal of the Vedic way is the restoration of our world, our communities, and ourselves to a sense of wholeness and wellbeing in balance with the Eternal Natural Law.

295

Never surrender yourself wholly to the will of another fallible human being. Finitude and imperfection are the primary distinguishing attributes of all human beings. To become perfect means to transcend humanness. Therefore, by definition, no illusioned human being is perfect, only those who have transcended their illusion.

296

True wisdom lies in knowing that everything is meaningful. Nothing is devoid of meaning – not even the most seemingly trivial or random of events. Learn to discern the hidden meanings behind all things, and you will have the keys to reality.

297

The greatest form of love consists of loyalty. Be loyal always toward those you love, and expect nothing less than reciprocal loyalty in return. Seek loyalty in your spouse, family and friends, and be likewise loyal to them.

298

Innocence is, without exception, the most precious quality that a human being can have. It is also, sadly, a quality that often leaves us open to immediate abuse by others. The key to happiness in life is to never reject innocence, while also never leaving oneself open to abuse at the hands of narcissists and psychopaths. Be both innocent and strong at the same time.

299

Truly meaningful progress and fulfillment never come about due to conflict with others. They come about due to the principles of wisdom, balance, and harmony with all that is of the nature of good. Conflict leads only to destruction. Harmony leads to creation. Seek harmony in yourself. Seek harmony between yourself and all other beings. Seek harmony between yourself and God. Harmony is made manifest in Dharma.

300

Atheism is for the weak-hearted. It is based upon the dread fear of surrender to an authority infinitely greater than ourselves. Spiritual pursuit is for those who are courageous. Spirituality is based upon the healthy acceptance that we are not beings of infinite authority.

301

The greatest paradox is this: The more you place yourself in the center of your concerns, the more anxiety you have. But the more you take yourself out of the center of your concerns, and place God in that center instead, the more you then find your true self and happiness. To find yourself, stop making yourself the center of all concern. The path of narcissism only leads to ignorance. Know that God is, and always was, the only true center of your reality.

302

The body changes with every moment. Our faces grow a bit older with each passing day. Emotions are as ephemeral as thin wisps of mist on a foggy morning. We change our minds all the time. Our intellects are constantly fluctuating – sometimes expanding, oftentimes contracting. Our false, egoic persona attaches itself to a different identity with each new life that it experiences. But our true self, the *atman*, is ever constant. Our true self is never-changing and is immortal. Never was there a time when it did not exist; and neither shall it ever cease to be. Know that you transcend the temporal and ever-changing body, emotions, mind, intellect and ego. Know that you are the true and eternal self that lies within and you will know perfect liberation.

303

The fact that you happen to be sitting in a chair at any given time is an example of factual knowledge. The reality that you are an eternal being, on the other hand, is of the nature of wisdom knowledge. To merely have an able grasp of facts and figures is to possess only factual knowledge. The accumulation of such quantitative data is a talent that even an inanimate computer has. Factual knowledge by it very essence is only knowledge of the temporary, the conditional, the situational and the ever changing. It is not knowledge of that which is eternal. Thus, it cannot be applied to issues of metaphysical, ontological, ethical or spiritual concern. Timeless wisdom, on the other hand, is knowledge that is always true at all places and at all times. It is knowledge that is neither relative, nor trivial. To have timeless wisdom is to know intuitively how to effectively use all forms of knowledge to manifest God's presence in all of your endeavors. Seek timeless wisdom, in addition to factual knowledge.

304

Never judge your own value merely upon the quantity of what you possess, but upon the quality of who you are. It is your quality that reveals your inner being.

305

Four important virtuous qualities that a good person must have are Simplicity, Humility, Devotion, and Compassion. Simplicity means knowing what is truly of value in life. Humility means being honest in your assessment of yourself in relation to others and in your relationship with God. Devotion means being aware of God's presence in your life, honoring the instructions of your guru, and exhibiting loyalty and fidelity to those who are above you. Compassion means feeling empathy upon seeing the pain of others, and then doing what is within your power to alleviate the pain of those who are suffering. Seek these four virtues as if they are the most precious of all jewels. Manifest these four qualities in your life, and you will know why you are alive.

306

We are currently experiencing a crisis of leadership in Sanatana Dharma. Truly authentic leaders are more difficult to find today than at any other time in human history. But there are a small handful of leaders who are actually authentic and who have integrity. We need to support Dharma by actively supporting those authentic leaders of the Vedic community who are themselves supporting Dharma. The support of such leaders needs to be practical and immediate. We need to donate funds, volunteer with any skill or talent we have, and help spread the teachings of such authentic leaders to the world. We also need to transform ourselves, with the direct empowerment of such pure *gurus*, to ourselves become able and authentic leaders of the Vedic community.

307

Honor - Duty - Nobility - Loyalty. These are the primary qualities of the *Dharma-Kshatriya*, the Dharma warrior. To have honor means to always do the right thing in any given context. There is no reason for self-respect without honor. To follow duty means to be faithful to our task whatever the personal cost to us may be. Nobility means always seeking excellence in all things. There is no second best; there is only either the very best, or there is failure. To have loyalty is to serve with faith and fidelity, never betraying our cause or our leaders within that cause. There is no one as fallen as he who betrays Dharma or the representatives of Dharma. With these four important qualities of honor, duty, nobility and loyalty as his most precious inner treasure, the contemporary Dharma warrior employs the boundless strength of his own being in the struggle for truth, justice and peace. It is better to perish in the pursuit of such higher ideals than to flee in the face of these ideals perishing before us. Such is the path of the Dharma warrior.

308

The grace of God is ever present. What is not ever present is our awareness of that divine grace. The more we cultivate that awareness, the more we know that everything in our life is always well and good. We are always living in an endless ocean of God's grace.

309

An inexperienced craftsman foolishly quarrels with his tools instead of seeing the fault in himself. The source of our unhappiness and of our joy lies only in our own vision of reality. We are the creators of our own suffering and happiness. We are the sole authors of our own destiny and experiences, and no one else. With every thought, every word, and every action that we produce, we are creating who and what we will be. We are free to either succeed or fail, to either rejoice or mourn. To blame any external factors for our present circumstances is the path of the fool. To accept that with our inherent freedom comes tremendous self-responsibility is the path of the wise.

310

If you must read, read the works of the ancient sages. If you must hear, hear the sounds of nature. If you must act, act with compassion toward all living beings. If you must create, create beauty that reflects the Eternal. If you must speak, speak the truth. If you must fight, fight for justice and Dharma. If you must die, die with inner calm and courage. If you must love (and love you must!), then love God, your fellow living beings, and God's natural creation with the entirety of your being.

311

Your outer form is a direct reflection of your inner sustenance. Your body and mental state are the direct result of whatever you eat and drink. Make sure to enjoy foods and drinks that are natural, organic, fresh, and rich in vitamins and nutrients. Do not make your body a graveyard of dead animals. A diet based upon death will only ultimately lead to death. Follow a healthy vegetarian diet - a diet based on life, not death.

312

What the senses take in, the mind in turn becomes. View images of beauty and sacredness, not ugliness and urban blight. Hear positive news about others, not gossip and negative complaints. Taste foods that promote life, not the dead flesh of animals. Smell the pleasing scents of nature, such as flowers, trees and the Earth. Feel the healing caress of those who love you. Your inner state will reflect the outer reality that your senses absorb. Only let the good in, and filter out the inauspicious. In this way, we become like unto that which our senses absorb.

313

False ego (*ahamkara*) systematically leads only to ignorance (*avidya*) through an inevitable causal chain. The stronger is the grip of your false ego, the more prominent is your self-centeredness. The more pronounced is your self-centeredness, the more exaggerated will your artificial desires be. The more exaggerated are your artificial desires, the greater will be your disappointment upon not fulfilling your desires. The greater your disappointment becomes, the more does anger overcomes you. Being blinded by anger, one falls easily under the deadly influence of self-delusion and ignorance. Transcend false ego and self-centeredness to know a life free from delusion and ignorance. The path to transcendence is found in the disciplined practice of Yoga spirituality alone.

314

You cannot always control when or how you will experience pleasure or pain. They come of their own accord, like the coming of the winter and summer seasons. But you can control how you will react to the presence of pleasure or pain. In both cases, consciously transcend the need to control. In transcending the need to control, you will automatically find yourself in control, and at peace. It is in acquiring such detached self-mastery that we find ultimate joy.

315

One of the most important powers that God has gifted you with is focus. If you can learn to focus all of your attentive energy like a laser beam, there will be no task, no goal, no dream that you cannot realize in this world. The uncontrolled chattering of your own mind is what is keeping you from focusing on your goals. Learn to still the mind, and you will gain the attentive focus that you need. It is through meditation alone that you will learn to still the mind.

316

Learn to use the power of discernment in all of your decisions, and never emotion, ego or envy. Discernment is having the ability to separate the truth from the untruth, the real from the unreal, the good from the deleterious, using the power of reason infused with wisdom. Discernment is a sharp sword with which you can separate what is truly in your best interest from that which only seems to be.

317

We must never confuse self-realization with self-absorption. The first has wisdom as its source; the second has selfishness as its source. The first has liberation as its result; the second has the bondage of further illusion as its result. Self-realization is the result we attain when we stop being self-absorbed.

318

Focus is the key to success and greatness. All of the greatest political leaders, religious leaders, *yogis*, military generals, and creative artists throughout world history shared in common an overwhelming power of focus. If we can learn to focus all of our attentive energy upon our goal, there is then nothing that we cannot accomplish.

319

Having a positive attitude does not mean that we have to be unrealistic about the realities of life in this world. Being realistic about the nature of our world, in turn, does not mean that we have to be in any way cynical. On the contrary, we are to be both positive and realistic simultaneously.

320

It is in listening that you gain knowledge. And knowledge is the most powerful possession that you can acquire. Fools are always speaking. But the wise know the power of listening - and learning.

321

In leading others, lead with wisdom and compassion. In following great people, follow with humility, dedication, honor and complete loyalty.

322

Know that you are never alone. God is always with you as your inner guide and as your closest friend. He is the silent, inner witness. He is the Supreme Self (Paramatman) in relation to our self (*atman*), the Soul of our soul, and the Sustainer of our being. Trust in God's, and know that you are always cared for from above.

323

In so many ways, the tree serves as an instructing *guru* toward us. The tree gives shelter to others, but asks little in return. It shows compassion. The tree stands strong and patient, regardless of the severity of weather it finds itself in. It has tolerance. The tree is silent, yet awes us with its dignity. It exhibits gravitas. The tree is beautiful, but it remains unaffected by all that happens around it. It has transcendent dispassion. The tree is our teacher. We must strive to learn from the tree, and to be as the tree.

324

Allow your own sincerity be the vehicle that carries you on the spiritual path. One cannot make any spiritual progress whatsoever without sincerity. Deep sincerity removes all obstacles on the journey towards truth.

325

A truly virtuous and noble person, whether it is a contemplative sage (*brahmana*) or a Dharma warrior (*kshatriya*), is motivated in his activities by a deep desire to protect those who are innocent and decent. His desire is to right the injustices carried out by malevolent people, and to bring tranquility and rejoicing to the hearts of good people. He will do this at any cost to his own safety or well-being. Indeed, it is true that there is no peace without justice. But more to the core of the issue, there is no justice without the inner peace and resolve of the righteous sage and warrior. The sage and the Dharma warrior constitute our greatest guarantors of justice.

326

Greed has no place in the spiritual domain whatsoever. Whether it is the 'Prosperity Gospel' preached by ethically corrupt televangelists, or the 'Law of Attraction' and 'The Secret' advocated by New Age scam-artists, God is not a money market manager. Spirituality does not exist in order to fulfill your every material whim or desire. Materialism is bondage. Spirituality serves to set us free from the bondage of materialism. Seek always to give, and not merely to take. Then, and only then, will you begin to experience the peace and joy of directly knowing the Divine. Aum Tat Sat.

327

Vegetarianism is an unassailably logical, rational and philosophically justifiable dietary lifestyle. Vegetarianism is healthy, ethical, economically just, and spiritually beneficial. If one choses not to be vegetarian, it is not because of any legitimate philosophical opposition to vegetarianism, but simply because one choses not to be vegetarian despite all reasonable evidence to be so. If one chooses to eat meat, it is because his base appetite has achieved victory over his intellect and reason.

328

The social domain must contain the spiritual element if it is to have any positive function or value. A society without spirituality at its center is a society that cannot secure the wellbeing of the people. It will be a demonic society, in which the government views the people as its slaves. A truly healthy society, on the other hand, will always be guided by Dharma. The government of such a Dharma Nation will view itself as the servant of the people, and will ensure that righteousness and justice abounds for all.

329

You are not God. You never were God. You never shall be God. Believing that you are God is precisely the cause of your false ego (*ahamkara*), which leads to your illusion (*maya*), and thus to your bondage (*bandha*) in ignorance (*avidya*). You are not God. You are a servant of God. Realize this eternal truth of your relationship to God as His humble servant with all of your being, and you will be well situated on the path to liberation.

330

By the very definition of the word 'politician' in modern usage, most politicians today are corrupt, self-serving and unethical. They have become a parasitic class of predators dedicated to taking from the people, rather than serving them. What the misguided political leaders of today need are spiritual advisors who will forcefully steer them in the direction of Dharma, justice, and the right course of action in all of their policy decisions. Such wise and able advisors are the *brahmanas*, the sagacious priestly scholars who once guided the Earth's leaders, but who are scarcely to be seen in today's society. *Brahmanas* are the teachers, spiritual guides, guardians of genuine culture, judges, and moral exemplars of all civilized societies. We need to reestablish the Brahmanical Order today if we are going to have such morally compelling advisors for our leaders. Only the unopposed leadership of such a Brahmanical Order can bring about the Vedic restoration that our Earth so desperately needs today. The creation of this Brahmanical Order is precisely the primary goal of the International Sanatana Dharma Society. We are a society of *brahmanas*.

331

Egotism, emotion and envy have become the three primary motivators in today's world. Egotism, emotion and envy are too often used as important decision-making factors for an increasing number of people in our current era. Our corrupt political leaders, using the engineered apparatus of the current distorted culture, have purposefully encouraged people to base their decisions and their actions upon these three factors alone. Thus, people now chose the course of their lives without the benefit of discernment and acquired wisdom. This abysmal situation only serves to benefit the corrupt politicians, and not the interests of the people. If we are to regain our freedom and spiritual dignity, we must learn to transcend the illusions of egotism, emotion and envy through the process of Yoga spirituality. Transcending these three poisons will free us both as individuals and as a people. Authentic Yoga spirituality is our path to freedom.

332

Vedic civilization encourages the cultivation of gardens, grottos and groves throughout society. Under a Dharma government, all urban blight will be systematically eliminated by creating such natural sanctuaries on every city block. It is in the beauty of such natural settings that even city folk can have some opportunity to experience the harmonizing effects of nature and the beauty of God.

333

Aum Namo Narayanaya. It is only in knowing Narayana (God) that we know ourselves. It is only in serving Narayana that we serve humanity. It is only in giving to Narayana that we give to the entire world. It is only in loving Narayana that we love all living beings. It is only in self-surrender to Narayana that we achieve the perfection of existence. Place only Sriman Narayana in the center of your life always if you are to know the true meaning of liberation. Jaya Sriman Narayana.

334

Access to Truth is open to all sincere people; but such access is tightly closed to all who do not transcend false ego. It is when you choose to create a brick wall of ego around yourself that you keep Truth out of your life. Remove your wall of false ego through Yoga, meditation, study of the Vedic scripture, and observing the teachings of a true *guru*, and allow Truth to come streaming in. Yoga *sadhana* (practice) is the process that tears down the wall of ego brick by brick.

335

The closer one gets to Truth, the smaller one's company necessarily becomes. While the Truth is for everyone, not everyone is for the Truth. Rather, the vast majority of living beings are not ready to know the Truth in its complete form. Truth is only for those rare souls who have the ability to surrender themselves to that Truth fully, without ego, without attachment to their own pet-theories or subjective prejudices. Only those who can approach Truth with humility, sincerity, devotion and great yearning will know Truth.

336

Before any man-made ideology existed, there was the Eternal Natural Way. For an everlasting duration of time after such ideologies, philosophies and theologies have disappeared from human memory, there will still be the Eternal Natural Way. Every other manmade ideology on Earth has failed us. We especially saw this throughout the history of the 20th century with its two ideologically based World Wars. The only path for changing the world in a total and meaningful way is through Vedic spirituality.

337

God is the supreme healer, and devotional meditation upon the Divine is our supreme medicine. If we water the root (God) of the tree of our lives with our devotion, then all the individual leaves of the tree (all of reality, including ourselves) are automatically nourished and healed. We water that divine root through our *sadhana* practice of devotional meditation upon the *mantra* Aum Namo Narayanaya. Our natural state is not one of suffering, but of health. True health becomes manifest when we restore our inherent state of balance and harmony with the Natural Order, or Dharma.

338

The greatest good that any *yogi*, Dharmi, or spiritual person can perform today is to work toward the preservation and restoration of Dharma. This is the most sattvic, or good, of activities that we can engage in. Dharma is the light of this world. Share the light of Dharma with all sentient beings in any way you can.

339

To love God is to embrace Dharma. And to embrace Dharma thoroughly and without reservation is what it truly means to be a *yogi*. Thus, the true *yogi* is a lover of God.

340

The most meaningful way to help others is to assist them to grow spiritually. The most effective way to help others in this spiritual way is to extend our utmost support to authentic spiritual teachers who have dedicated their lives to enlightening others. It is in helping such Dharma leaders that we exponentially increase our own efforts to bring spiritual relief to the world world. Serve the true *guru* in his mission to save the world and you have helped all!

341

Consciousness is not an 'it'. Concsiousness is not an inert object. Rather, consciousness is an 'I' (*aham*). It is a living subject. It is an 'I' from its own perspectival sense of self-awareness, and a 'thou' (*tvam*) when objectively viewed from the perspective of another locus (*svarupam*) of consciousness. Consciousness is non-distinct from personality. Consciousness is personality. Impersonalism is, thus, directly the denigration of consciousness. Impersonalism renders consciousness into insentiency (*jadatva*). It is for this reason that the Vedic scriptures reject impersonalism, and embrace personalism. The Vedic path is the way of consciousness and personality.

342

Consciousness, seen in the most general of philosophical senses, is both one and many in accordance with what precise aspect of 'consciousness' we are referring to. Consciousness is one in qualitative terms, but it is also many in quantitative terms. In the latter (the many), it is precisely the inherent personality factor of consciousness per se (in and of itself) that gives consciousness the ability to be multiple - God being the supreme expression of personality. All the individual units of finite consciousness represent the many. We are all individual *atmans*. God represents the one. He is Param-atman (the Supreme Atman), the one Supreme Atman who is the source of all other *atmans*.

343

We are eternal beings currently undergoing a temporal, material experience. While we witness everything around us coming into being, and eventually disappearing into nonbeing, we ourselves have never been born and will never die. Nothing can harm us. Nothing can kill us. When we fully realize our inherently eternal nature, we then lose all fear of death or loss. Thus, the *yogi* is the most courageous and fearless of all people. The *yogi* can accomplish any goal fearlessly.

344

The currently reigning dogma of Radical Egalitarianism, and the congruent myth of equality, represent the predominant force propelling the Kali Yuga forward on its destructive path. They are the very engine of cultural degeneration that has led to our current psychosocial state of spiritual emptiness and dissatisfaction. Every ancient wisdom-tradition on Earth has taught that no two human beings are equal; no two people are the same. We are all unique and nonreplicable personalities. It is only in accurately understanding the natural, hierarchical significance of each and every distinct person, concept and object in the cosmos that we can fully grasp the nature of the whole. Radical Egalitarianism leads to the mediocrity, ugliness, dumbing down of the general populace, political corruption, and pandering to the lowest common denominator that has become central to today's culture. To seek personal excellence and nobility, on the other hand, is the essence of the Vedic way.

345

In the beginning, there was *Veda*. *Veda* is transcendental knowledge that is non-distinct from the Absolute. Being non-distinct from the Absolute, *Veda* is eternal. It has never come into being; it will never go out of being. Before there was a manifest material cosmos, there was *Veda*. Before the formation of our planet, there was *Veda*. Before the birth of nations and empires, there was *Veda*. Before there were religions, there was *Veda*. When all things have finally ceased to be, there will still be *Veda*. Take shelter in the eternal, transcendent Truth. Take shelter in *Veda*.

346

There are four principles of character that all followers of Dharma must strive to achieve if they wish to have lives that are successful and joyous. These are: 1) Discipline, 2) Excellence, 3) Nobility, and 4) Perfection. While at one time it was universally understood that it was crucial to cultivate these four qualities in one's life, these four words have now become nearly blasphemy in the modern world. Indeed, much of modern society seems to purposefully encourage the very opposite of these four values. We are encouraged now to celebrate mediocrity. This is, however, only due to ignorance of what these four words actually mean. Discipline means having the strength and freedom of self-mastery; being in control of your body, emotions, mind, intellect and ego. Excellence means bringing everything that you do to its qualitative best, rather than settling for mediocrity or for merely what is 'good enough'. To celebrate nobility is to live a life of honor and truth, and to make your word your bond. Perfection does not involve an attempt to imitate another person's virtues, but to bring your own unique inner virtues to their maximal expression. The Dharmi strives at all times to make these four virtues manifest in his or her life.

347

An essential challenge that many spiritual seekers face on their journey is in learning how to focus upon the path. Many seekers go in several different directions at once in their spiritual search, thus dividing their attention and energies. While it is always wise to explore as much as possible early on in one's spiritual life, eventually one does need to begin to filter out that which is inferior if the goal is to actually know the superior. It is only through the necessary process of rejecting that which we have seen to be illusory opinions or practices along the way that we can then find the true and eternal path.

348

The true sage conducts his presence among us in such a manner that makes it clear to those with the eyes to see that he is not firmly a part of this realm. His connection to the material is exceedingly tenuous. He, in actuality, traverses two planes simultaneously, with one foot in the material and one in the spiritual. He is physically manifest only with the purpose of delivering access to those who need proximity to his illumination. His physical presence here is an expression of his grace toward us such that he can give us a glimpse of a much higher realm. He subsists in this material world only to serve as a portal to those higher realms. Thus the true sage is a sacred bridge of mercy here to help those who are entrapped within the material realm to access spiritual reality. Such is the unseen and mysterious nature of the true *guru.* Like a flash of lightning in the sky, he will all too soon be gone.

349

More so than any other single attributive factor, you know a true leader by the degree of his or her personal character and integrity. The greatest leader has the greatest depth of character. A so-called leader who is lacking in character is not a leader at all. That deep and abiding character, in turn, must be attributable to the leader's total reliance upon the wisdom and guidance of the ancient ways. The leader's world-view, leadership style and personal behavior must be a reflection of the eternal traditional ways. It is in fidelity to eternal Dharma that true character is rooted.

350

Atheism is not an honestly held philosophical stance. Like the disease of obesity or the venal indulgence of boredom, atheism is no more than a symptom of excessive luxury and extravagance in a dying society. It is only when a culture of intellectual decadence, complaisant self-pleasure and lethargy overtake a given population that atheism begins to flourish as the pseudo-philosophical stance of the lazy and corrupt elite of any society. Atheism is not an intellectual position; it is symptom of spiritual and moral atrophy.

351

True and authentic Vedic spirituality has historically rejected all tamasic (dark and ignorance-based) behavior and worldviews. The tamasic attitude is easily recognized by its infamous celebration of evil, amorality, egotism, selfishness, cruelty, 'beyond good and evil' delusions, manipulation, exploitation, abuse of others and circumvention of the principles of Dharma. The tamasic lifestyle is known in ideological form as Asura-Marga in Sanskrit, or the Path of the Demonic. It is also known in modern neo-occult circles as the so-called 'Left-Hand Path', as well as Thelema, Crowleyianism, Luciferianism, Satanism, and by other cultic names. Such psychopathic ideologies attempt to proffer a pseudo-philosophical justification for the warped mental state of narcissistic sociopathy. It is the religion of *ahamkara*, of false ego. Thus, it falls under the general category of atheism, since it is the attempt to replace the Divine with the 'god' of ego. Asura-Marga is also the psychological foundation of Abrahamism. While not all narcissistic sociopaths are necessarily conscious followers of the 'Left-Hand Path', all serious followers of the 'Left-Hand Path' are by definition narcissistic sociopaths. This destructive path is in every way the mirror opposite of Dharma. There is no reconciliation between Dharma and *adharma*.

352

To thoughtlessly denigrate our historic past is to callously maltreat our very own ancestors, those who are responsible for our very existence in this world. The modernist ideology of socio-historical progressivism has falsely convinced too many of us that the inhabitants of the past were necessarily less intelligent, less moral, less sophisticated, more superstitious and less rational than we are today. In an overwhelming number of cases, however, the very opposite of this false narrative was the truth. Such shortsighted temporocentrism has given us an unwarranted and inaccurate sense of superiority toward our ancestors that we must learn to overcome if we are to learn from their immense wisdom. Our ancestors and our historic past are sources of wisdom, inspiration and strength for us today.

353

'Hierarchy' has become one of the dirtiest words imaginable in our present era. 'Hierarchy', however, is nothing more than a description of a natural and beneficial phenomenon. Hierarchy is a rational accounting of the natural succession of qualitative degrees in any given category of reality that is designed to provide intellectual coherency to our empirical experiences of the world around us. Everything falls under one or more sets of categories, including ideas, states of being, living beings, persons and measurable differentiations of every description. Hierarchy is not 'oppressive', 'backward', or 'unfair'. Hierarchy is an inherent and indispensible aspect of nature. There is no nature, and thus no coherent world, without hierarchy. Thus hierarchy is a beneficial part of life.

354

While followers of Dharma fully acknowledge the important role that *karma*, genetic and cultural heredity, environment and other external factors play in shaping our lives, we also strongly stress the importance of personal responsibility. We are the principal authors of our present circumstances, and not merely external conditions alone. We have created who and what we are in the present moment. We are not victims of fate, of society, of 'unfairness', or of any other external forces. We are free personalities, who freely choose our own states of being. Only a bad workman argues foolishly with his tools, when he should in actuality be arguing with his own lack of skill. It is only in acknowledging complete responsibility over our own lives that we are fully expressing our freedom.

355

Honor your ancestors. Honor your family's past. Honor your people's achievements. Honor what once was. Do not denigrate your ancestral past or be ashamed of your ancestral past. Only then will you be fully worthy of your present life.

356

Look all around you. Travel this Earth and try your best to fill your eyes and your senses with as much as you can take in. Sriman Narayana is the origin and foundation of all that. Travel to other universes, what to speak of other stars. Sriman Narayana is the origin and foundation of all that. Think any thought that you are capable of thinking. Read all of the world's literature containing all human ideas from the very beginning of time. Of all things that are conceptual, Sriman Narayana is the origin and foundation of all that. This is the Divine to Whom we surrender.

357

Vaishnavas (devotees of Sriman Narayana) are to couple our humility with healthy self-confidence, our reserve with fearlessness, and our service attitude with the responsibility of being society's leaders. For this reason, the terms '*dasa*' and '*dasi*' (the respective masculine and feminine terms for 'servant') are no longer to be used in the initiated names of devotees. The critical needs of our age demand that devotees be strong, courageous, assertive and in command. In their inner spiritual mood, devotees must always be servants (*dasa/dasi*). But in practical action, devotees must act as leaders (*nayakas*).

358

The Rasa Lila is one of the most misunderstood aspects of Krishna's divine play. Whereas at one time only the most advanced *yogis* meditated upon the deep, inner meaning of the Rasa Lila, now you can go to any Indian grocery store and buy cheap posters depicting this divine mystery! Early Vaishnavism did not emphasize this aspect of Sri Krishna's pastimes upon the earth. Rather, Krishna was celebrated as a teacher, an *avatara*, a restorer of Dharma, and a punisher of those who opposed Dharma. It has only been in recent centuries that the Rasa Lila has been overemphasized more than any other aspect. The Rasa Lila is an extremely esoteric and mystical phenomenon that one is meant to contemplate only once one has completely transcended all material sexual desire. It is a *lila* that is as much metaphorical as anything else. It is symbolic of the central place that God has in all reality. The vast majority of people are not meant to contemplate the Rasa Lila. Rather, we should meditate upon Krishna the King, the Warrior, the Avatara, etc. It is the Krishna of the *Bhagavad Gita* that represents the primary form of Krishna whom we should be worshiping.

359

Beginning several centuries after the disappearance of Gautama Buddha, the leaders of the Buddhist movement began to wander away from his pure teachings. Hence we have the post-Buddha dogma that states that there is no eternal self. The Buddha himself never taught this. Rather, he taught that anything that is transitory is not the true self. The Buddha taught that we are presently in a state of suffering, and that we consequently need *nirvana*, or enlightenment, to bring our suffering to an end. But if there is no self, as many present-day Buddhist leaders claim, then who is it that is suffering and who is it that needs enlightenment? The self-contradicting dogma that there is no eternal self undermines the principle teaching of the Buddha himself.

360

Those who work toward the creation of a Dharma Nation are opposed to many of the presuppositions of both the traditional Left and the traditional Right. We reject the rampant sex and drug culture, the self-centeredness and the anti-intellectualism of the Left. We also reject the cultural incuriousness, the bourgeois materialism and the unenlightened closed-mindedness of the Right. A Dharma Nation would be predicated neither upon the principles of the Left nor upon those of the Right, but upon principles that are eternal, natural and spiritual.

361

Sexuality is one of the most mysterious, fundamental and formidable forces operative among all living beings within the material domain. It is a double-edged sword that represents potentially both the very best and the very worst of vitalic energies. Guided by Dharma and the desire to express true love, sexuality is a natural and loving expression of one soul toward another. Never settle for anyone less than your true soul mate. Understood in this way, sexuality can be a pure spiritual expression of dynamic love. But when misguided by selfishness, lust and the desire for exploitation, that very same sexuality becomes a monstrous expression of destructive ego, and can lead to the abuse and objectification of others. For this reason, sexuality must always be carefully approached with the proper respect that this spiritual force deserves. Always let the Dharmic principle of monogamous loving relationship, and not the egoic desire for domination, be your guide in all sexual matters.

362

Do not strive merely to be different. Strive to be great.

363

Skilled laborers represent the sturdy legs of society. They create the practical foundation upon which civilization is built. Without their hard work, masterfully wielded skills and craftsmanship, society would be incapable of functioning. For this reason, the dignity of skilled labor must always be honored and respected by all other segments of society. All skilled workers should be encouraged to organize themselves into non-political guilds in which the various crafts are represented in order to encourage fellowship and the apprenticeship of future generations of dedicated workers. In this way, workers will take well-deserved pride in their craftsmanship. There is no human dignity without work.

364

Very sadly, most Indian Hindus today have been encouraged by their misguided leaders to be more India-centric than Dharma-centric. Hindutva and Hindu Nationalism, however, have very little to do with Sanatana Dharma. While national pride is a positive characteristic that should always be encouraged among all people, India is just one nation of many. It is not the 'birthplace' of Sanatana Dharma. Sanatana Dharma, by its very definition, is universal and eternal. It transcends any specific and temporal nation-state – including India. Sanatana Dharma Vijayate.

365

The greatest, most excellent, or most superlative mode of being in any given field or category can necessarily only refer to one particular person, and not to several. There is only one person within Reality who is the most beautiful, or the strongest, or the wisest, or the most compassionate, or the most fearless, or the most good, etc. When we finally encounter that one living being who possesses the maximally superlative positive attributes in every single category, and who has those auspicious attributes to an infinite degree, we have then encountered the Supreme Absolute, Sriman Narayana, above Whom there is no one.

366

If you approach the *guru* already eager to be a *guru* yourself, then you are barely worthy of even calling yourself a good disciple. Desire, instead, to be a good disciple. A true *guru* does not wish to be a *guru*. Rather, he has no choice but to be one.

367

To ensure that we remain upon the spiritual path without deviation, our focus should be on fidelity. We must have fidelity to the instructions of the true and authentic *guru*. We must have fidelity to the guidance of the Shastra (Vedic scriptures). We must have fidelity to our goal of achieving loving devotion toward the lotus feet of Bhagavan Sri Krishna. It is precisely when a spiritual practitioner does not have such fidelity that he strays into the realm of subjective speculation rather than remaining upon the path of clear spiritual assurance. There is no spiritual progress without fidelity.

368

Do not look for justice in government. Do not look for fairness in legislation. Do not look for culture in Hollywood, or for accurate news in the media. Do not look for truth and objectivity in academia. Do not look for meaningful fellowship on the Internet. Do not look for love in a bar. Do not look for enlightenment in a drug. You will never find the real in the unreal. Only the words of the enlightened masters can reveal what is real to us.

369

The very essence of Yoga consists of controlling one's mind-substance through focused meditative awareness upon Sriman Narayana.

370

A *Brahmana* (a person with an inherently philosophical, spiritual and sattvic nature) is above all a guardian of Vedic culture. *Brahmanas* are known for their very good memory. They are traditionally known to memorize extremely large sections of the Vedic literature, thus becoming living scriptures in order to preserve this sacred literature for the benefit of future generations. More symbolically, *brahmanas* serve as the memory of the people. When society as a whole begins to forget the true nature and purpose of Dharma, it is the *brahmanas* who remember. They are the memory repositories of Vedic truth. When the people have been led away from the path of Dharma, it is the *brahmanas* who remind the people of what it means to live a life that is in harmony with the Natural Order, a life of ultimate meaning. The time has now come for such *brahmanas* to once again lead the people onto the path of Dharma.

371

Our critique of the Indian movement known as 'Hindu Nationalism' is a straightforward one. Hindu Nationalists view themselves as Indian first, and as followers of Sanatana Dharma second. Dharma Nationalists, on the other hand, are followers and practitioners of Sanatana Dharma first, foremost and always. Our primary identity is rooted in Dharma, with all other correlating identities being secondary. We are not Hindu Nationalists. We are Dharma Nationalists.

372

To meditate upon a *mantra* is infinitely more effective and meaningful than merely chanting a *mantra.* A computer can be programed to chant a *mantra.* A parrot can be trained to chant a *mantra.* To merely chant is primarily a vocal activity. But meditation upon a *mantra* is to purposefully engage one's mind and inner landscape completely in the *mantra's* essential sonic nature. To meditate upon a *mantra* is to willingly focus one's attentive awareness upon the *mantra* in such a way as to allow oneself to be inwardly transformed by the *mantra's* inherent spiritual power. Thus, we should meditate upon the transcendental names of God and be happy.

373

Do not allow your political stance to contaminate your spirituality. Rather, allow your spirituality to inform your politics.

374

For those who are sincerely on the spiritual path, a deep sense of humility is everything. Humility is the most empowering quality that the *yogi* can have.

375

A true *guru* (*sadguru*) is not just a teacher, but is also a trainer and a guide in *sadhana.* He has the ability to both guide his students in Vedantic enquiry, as well as in their pursuit of deeper levels of *sadhana* (spiritual practice). The qualified *guru* can guide his disciples in the shedding of their *anarthas* (deep psychological and ethical faults) and *samskaras* (previous traumas impressed upon the psyche), in the positive cultivation of their noble and spiritual character, and in deepening their blissful experience within their *sadhana* practice. It is in bringing closely together both knowledge and practice that the student can witness actual spiritual progress. Only a true and authentic *guru* can facilitate such an empowering process.

376

Demonic persons desire the power of the gods, but without the moral responsibility of the gods. Thus, they end up with neither.

377

It is very true that a real leader has 100% control over their speech and what they say. They never speak without first thinking about what they are saying, whose ears it is for, the context that they find themselves in, etc. Having such self-control is what it means to be a leader.

378

The warrior and the *yogi* are very similar. The inner qualities that are necessary to be a victorious warrior and to be a successful *yogi* are one and the same. A perfect warrior is a servant of Dharma. The perfect *yogi* has the strength and the courage of a warrior. The perfection of both the martial path and the way of the spiritual practitioner finds its culmination in the Dharma Warrior.

379

Spirituality cannot be merely thought about, but is only truly understood when fully experienced. We experience spiritual reality most directly only when we deeply practice spirituality. It is for this reason that performing our daily *sadhana* (spiritual discipline) is of such importance. When we find, however, that it is sometimes a difficult struggle to keep up with our daily practice, we must never use such challenges as a cause for guilt or feelings of failure. Instead, just begin again the next day. Allow the sweetness of meditation upon the holy names of God to positively attract us to performing our daily *sadhana*, and never the bitterness of guilt. May our meditation be always sweet.

380

A truly authentic man cherishes women with all of his heart. But in his core biological essence, he never ceases to be a man. A truly authentic woman loves men with all of her heart, and never sees men as her enemy.

381

When we think about the process of meditation, we tend to envision three elements: ourselves as the meditator, the mantra upon which we are meditating, and the meditative experience itself. There is, however, a fourth element to meditation. That fourth element is God, who is the ultimate goal of all true and authentic meditation. It is in the ecstasy of devotional meditation that we experience God directly and intimately in the form of a reciprocal, loving relationship. In this way, we should understand that the meditative experience is not merely a process, but a relationship. It is only in these terms of transcendental personalism and eternal relationship that we can understand the highest significance of meditation.

382

America is a nation that is full of earnest, noble and giving people. The American nation was originally founded upon the notions of liberty and justice. But America's rulers have viciously betrayed both the American people and the founding principles of our nation, and have savagely exploited the very best of what America has been for their own corrupt and selfish gain. The time has now arrived for the people to reclaim our original American nation, to annihilate the miscreant tyrants who have thrived on our blood for so many generations, and to restore America to the greatness that she has been deprived of. Only a full national restoration of what the American nation was at her founding will guarantee that America will continue to be for a thousand generations into the future.

383

For the last several decades, Yoga and Vedic spirituality have been falsely associated with pacifism, New Age irrationalism, the hippie lifestyle and effeminacy. This has been a deliberate and conscious attempt by the demonic elite to separate Vedic culture from its distinctively warrior roots. Vedic culture was always steeped in the warrior ethos. It has always been a tradition that has encouraged strength, courage and martial excellence in its practitioners. The time has now come to abandon the weakness falsely ascribed to the Vedic tradition, and to re-embrace our Dharma warrior ethos. It is now time for the Dharma Warrior to be reborn.

384

Men can strive to be masculine, while at the same time being gentle. Women can strive to be feminine, while at the same time being strong. To truly acknowledge the natural inclinations of our specific gender means that we must also honor the most important characteristics of what it means to be noble (*arya*) and human (*manushya*).

385

One would be unwise, indeed, to mistake the *guru* as merely being a man or a woman, an Indian or an American, or as being in any manner related to the physical form. The *guru* is pure consciousness, operating as pure consciousness, through the medium of physicality. The true *guru* transcends all material designations. It is only in knowing this fact that one will be eligible to approach the true *guru* and to benefit from such a *guru's* presence.

386

Everyone is a spark of the Divine.
Very few are stars.
There is only one ultimate Sun.

387

You will never be in a position to help the world in any real way, or to even help save yourself and your family, until you finally come to the realization that the many problems, sufferings and crises that our world is currently experiencing are not accidental. Our social, political and economic suffering has been purposefully imposed upon us by the conscious and malevolent design of an evil elite. Until you quickly awaken to this incontrovertible fact, you are powerless to affect positive change.

388

To be one who is devoted to truth is all too often a solitary path.

389

Whenever a good person is attacked by enemy detractors, such cowardly attacks only make the good person stronger, wiser, more agile in combatting the enemy, and more determined to achieve total victory. In this way, the more the enemy detractors attack the good person, the more they are actually doing him a favor – and ensuring their own inevitable destruction at his hands.

390

If you support, or in any way acquiesce to, the New World Order, globalization, or the deconstruction of traditional cultures and ways of being, then you cannot claim simultaneously to be a 'spiritual' person. If you do not know what these terms even fully mean, then you have a duty as a spiritual person to educate yourself on their meanings as soon as possible. The activities of the New World Order represent the deadliest enemy of Dharma today.

391

Any man who thinks that all women as a gender are his enemy is, in actuality, his own greatest enemy. Any woman who thinks that all men as a gender are her enemy is, in actuality, her own greatest enemy. Healthy minded men and women are indispensable to each other. They complete each other. They are as inseparable from one another as is the sunshine from the sun.

392

Evil is always parasitic in its essential nature. Evil is never self-sustaining. It is always empty. Thus, it is completely dependent upon cynically exploiting the energy, enthusiasm and hard work of innocent people in order to support its own sinister agenda. Evil can only exploit the energy of others, however, if it does so while hidden behind a veil of secrecy, illusion and lies. The most effective means for defeating evil is to deprive it of its sources of sustenance. The parasite must be deprived of its food. Expose the fact that the purveyors of evil have been thriving by sucking the blood of the people for multiple generations, and the people will turn upon evil. Starve evil, and evil will be defeated.

393

Every time that a criminal is given leniency, the opposite of compassion has then triumphed. Each time that a murderer is given any sentence less firm than the death penalty, compassion has been mocked. Whenever unrepentant evil has been prematurely forgiven, compassion has been betrayed. Compassion is being misused whenever it furthers injustice. Compassion is not an emotion or a feeling. Compassion is not a response rendered from a place of weakness. Rather, true compassion is synonymous with justice. It is only when we are acting as a result of a character that is based upon strength that we are acting in true compassion. If you wish to be compassionate, then be strong.

394

Truth never seeks unity with untruth, but only seeks unity unto itself.

395

Never surrender yourself to passing pseudo-cultural fads perpetuated by a malevolent media.

396

Neither the gods and goddesses (*devas* and *devis*), nor the demonic beings (*asuras*), who are described in the Vedic scriptures are to be understood to be merely symbolic. The theory that they are just symbolic is reflective of New Age inspired psychologism, and not authentic spirituality. Traditional spirituality explains that these are beings with as much reality, personality, and free will as are possessed by all human beings. Such beings are personalities, and are thus as real as you are. These beings are very real. The gods and goddesses are benevolent beings who we are to welcome into our lives and cooperate with. The demonic beings are malevolent entities who we are to avoid at all costs if we wish to avoid suffering, delusion and bondage. The path of Vedic spirituality gives us clear guidance on how to cultivate good, and how to avoid evil in our lives.

397

Too many people mistake arrogance for intelligence. The two are, in actuality, mirror opposites of one another. Arrogance is born from the illusion of ego. Transcending the illusion of ego is born from cultivating true intelligence (*jnana*). Arrogance is a clear sign of the lack of true intelligence.

398

The liberated sage is the best friend and the greatest benefactor of all living beings. It is through the teachings of such a liberated sage in the form of the *guru* that the human person is provided with a clear and reliable roadmap in his journey toward Truth. It is in the living example seen in the activities of the liberated sage that the spiritual aspirant perceives Dharma in action. It is by the compassionate grace of the liberated sage that the fallen populace of our current era is given the ability to rise above the ignorance of our age, and to experience firsthand the bliss of the Eternal. In the Kali Yuga, tragically, the very opposite of this understanding of the nature of the *guru* has now become the norm. Such divine sages are no longer recognized in our degraded age as being the greatest of friends, but are often misperceived to be enemies. In the Kali Yuga, rather than honoring and celebrating the rare opportunity to grow in the light of such sages, we instead fear the *guru*, hate the *guru*, are suspicious of the *guru*, and in some instances when the monstrous ego feels especially threatened, even desire to kill the *guru*. Such was the fate of a Socrates and a Jesus, among other great sages, within the history of the Kali Yuga. The only so-called *'guru'* that is acceptable today is found in the malevolent guidance of one's own illusioned ego. If you are reading this now within the historical confines of the Kali Yuga, seek out what remaining liberated sages are still accessible to you in this dark era, and surrender at the feet of such a being. It is only in consciously countering the enervating influence of the Kali Yuga that you will know true and lasting enlightenment.

399

The core root of all forms of authentic spirituality consists in learning to fully and without self-involved motivation love someone outside of just your own self. It is only when you learn how to love another selflessly, and that you actively practice such selfless love of others, that you have truly begun the first steps on your spiritual journey.

400

The inherent ability to engage in the philosophic enterprise is not an equal opportunity capacity. Among the general human population, a very small number of individuals actually possess the necessary intellectual discipline and discursive ability to think truly philosophically. Three of the most important intellectual qualities that are indispensible in order to operate on the philosophical level are discernment (*duradrshti*), discrimination (*viveka*) and discretion (*suniti*). Discernment is the ability to understand the true nature of either a truth-claim or of a perceivable phenomenon beyond the mere surface level presented to one's cognitive and perceptual faculties. Discrimination is the intellectual ability to detect, acknowledge and understand objective differences between objects, concepts and individuals that make up a whole, along with the ability to correctly categorize these items in accordance with their inherent hierarchical value. Discretion is the acquired aptitude of knowing what is appropriate, beneficial and advantageous to think, say or do within a given circumstance in accordance with one's present social company, personal responsibilities and goals. Under no circumstances should philosophical judgments ever be based upon emotion, sentiment or an infantile desire for personal wish fulfillment.

Opinions that are based upon emotions alone are the very opposite of philosophically conclusive (*siddhanta*). Thus, emotionalism is directly antithetical to philosophy. The vast majority of persons within the Kali Yuga base their opinions upon their ephemeral emotional states. Only a very few actually base their conclusions upon true philosophy.

Index

The index is organized by aphorism number.

About the Author

Sri Dharma Pravartaka Acharya is a European-American who was born in New York City. He has been practicing Sanatana Dharma and Yoga spirituality for over 43 years, and teaching this path to others since 1988.

His dedicated interest in self-realization began when he first read the *Bhagavad Gita*, the most important philosophical text of the Dharma tradition, at the tender age of ten. A philosophically inquisitive child, Sri Acharyaji proceeded to collect and read a vast number of books relating to Vedic spirituality and Yoga. He also began to practice various forms of Yoga, *pranayama* (breathing exercises) and meditation soon after this first encounter with the *Gita.*

At the young age of 14, Sri Acharyaji visited a Hindu temple for the first time in Queens, New York. So awed was he with the majestic beauty and spiritual power that he encountered in this temple that, on the spot, he decided to devote his life to preserving the path of Vedic spirituality. After living the highly disciplined life of a celibate Hindu monk for over six years, Sri Acharyaji was ordained as an orthodox Hindu *brahmana* (a spiritual teacher and priest) in India in 1986.

Acharyaji went on to earn a B.A. in philosophy from Loyola University Chicago, as well as an MA and a Ph.D. from the University of Wisconsin-Madison. When his Ph.D. advisor tried to persuade Acharyaji to eventually become a professor, Acharyaji made the impassioned reply that "I don't want to study the history of religion. I want to make religious history." He has been doing just that ever since.

Sri Acharyaji is the Founder-Acharya of the International Sanatana Dharma Society, a growing global movement designed to teach the truth of Vedic spirituality to the world.

He has lectured as an invited authority on Dharma at dozens of top American universities, such as Harvard, Columbia, Rutgers, Cornell, and Northwestern. He has also served as a consultant for such Fortune 500 companies as Ford Motor Corporation and Lucent Technology.

Sri Acharyaji was the Resident Acharya (Spiritual Preceptor) of the Hindu Temple of Nebraska from 2007-2009, which represents the first time in American history that a Hindu temple had ever made such an esteemed appointment.

Sri Acharyaji is currently recognized as one of the world's foremost scholars on the Yoga tradition, Dharma and meditation, as well as being a truly authentic and self-realized spiritual teacher (*guru*).

Sri Dharma Pravartaka Acharya is universally acclaimed as one of the world's most respected and qualified Dharma teachers and leaders. Dr. Deepak Chopra exclaimed about Sri Acharyaji in 2002:

"*You've done truly phenomenal work teaching the pure essence of Yoga*".

In a similar manner, Dr. David Frawley has said about Sri Acharyaji,

"*Sri Acharyaji represents the Sankalpa [the will] of the Hindu people and the cause of Sanatana Dharma. I urge all Hindus everywhere to give him your full support, assistance, and encouragement in his crucial work. He needs and deserves our help.*"

Sri Acharyaji has the support and encouragement of many hundreds of the world's most respected Vedic *guru*, leaders and teachers.

With a very large international following of both traditional Indian Hindus and Western Yoga practitioners, Sri Acharyaji is especially renowned for his highly authentic approach to spirituality, his authoritative and scholarly method of teaching, and his clear emphasis on serious spiritual practice and direct experience of self-realization.

Sri Acharyaji's teachings stress the achievement of enlightenment through the dedicated practice of meditation, Yoga, and directly experiencing the presence of the Divine. Another overarching aspect of Sri Acharyaji's teachings focuses on the importance of love, compassion and service toward all living beings.

Whether speaking to an audience of thousands, or having a heart-felt discussion with only one person, Sri Acharyaji vividly conveys a deeply moving sense of personal compassion, peace, humility, and spiritual insight that has endeared him to thousands of students and admirers throughout the world.

For more information on the life and teachings of Sri Dharma Pravartaka Acharya, please visit:

www.dharmacentral.com

What is the International Sanatana Dharma Society?

The International Sanatana Dharma Society (ISDS) is a global spiritual movement dedicated to practicing and teaching the ancient Vedic religious tradition in its fully authentic and unaltered form. Our goal in spiritual practice is to accept no watering-down or compromises to the time-honored integrity of the Vedic philosophy and lifestyle. The only way to practice and truly benefit from Dharma spirituality is to practice Dharma on its own sacred terms, and not merely as a further extension of our ego (*ahamkara*).

Our religion is known in the Sanskrit language as Sanatana Dharma, or the Eternal Natural Way. We thus call ourselves "Dharmis", or followers of Dharma. Members of the ISDS follow Sanatana Dharma exclusively as their chosen religious path. We do not mix and match pure Vedic spirituality with any other religious traditions, modern "new age" innovations, or pop spirituality. We exclusively identify with, and practice, Sanatana Dharma as our path to Self-realization and God-consciousness.

We know truth by means of a) the instructing words and guidance of the enlightened Guru (Guru-vani), b) the guidance of the revealed Vedic scriptures (Shastra-pramana), and c) the use of our own reasoning faculties (*vichara*), philosophical discernment (*viveka*) and personal experience (*anubhava*). Sanatana Dharma is not a religion of blind faith, fanaticism, or wishful thinking. It is a religion of acquired spiritual/philosophical wisdom, coupled with direct personal experience of the transformative presence of God.

The teachings and practices of the ISDS are based directly upon the Vedic scriptures. Our scriptures consist of the entire *shruti* and *smriti* cannons of the Vedic literature, but with special emphasis on the teachings of the *Bhagavad Gita*, *Upanishads*, *Bhagavata Purana*, *Vishnu Purana*, *Brahma Sutras*, *Yoga Sutras* and *Narada Bhakti Sutras.*

Aum Tad Vishnu Paramam Padam

> "The abode of Vishnu is the highest state of existence." - *Rig Veda*, 1:22:20

Members of the ISDS recognize the Vedic scriptures' clear declaration that Sriman Narayana (also known as Vishnu) represents the supreme form of Godhead (Brahman), and we express special devotion to the *avatara* of Sriman Narayana for this age: Bhagavan Sri Krishna and His divine consort (*divya-shakti*) Srimati Radharani. Sri Krishna was on the earth over 5100 years ago, and is the speaker of the famous *Bhagavad Gita*, the most important scripture for our current age. The meaning of life is to revive our innate devotional consciousness (*bhakti*) toward the Supreme Godhead, and to reunite ourselves with Sriman Narayana in eternal loving union.

Our spiritual practice (*sadhana*) consists of the full classical Yoga system (*ashtanga*) permeated throughout with a consciousness of *bhakti* (devotion). *Bhakti*, or devotional consciousness, is understood to be both the highest means of liberation, as well as the ultimate goal of spiritual life and culture. Thus, *bhakti* is not merely the most effective means (*upaya*) for spiritual liberation; it is also the ultimate goal (*paramartha*) of life. Members of the ISDS all strive to achieve Self-realization (*atma-jnana*), leading finally to God-consciousness (*brahma-vidya*).

Our primary form of meditation is *mantra* meditation upon the divine sound vibration:

Aum Namo Narayanaya

The founder and spiritual preceptor (Acharya) of the ISDS is Sri Dharma Pravartaka Acharya, who is more popularly known as Sri Acharyaji. He is widely recognized throughout the leadership of the global Hindu community as one of the most authentic, knowledgeable and visionary Hindu teachers on the world stage today. Members of the ISDS acknowledge Sri Acharyaji as a truly enlightened sage, as a Sad-guru (true *guru*) capable of guiding his disciples to the deepest realization of wisdom and spiritual liberation, and all members strive to follow his spiritual teachings in our daily lives with sincerity, loyalty and fidelity.

Distinctly Authentic Approach to Vedic Spirituality

There are several features that make the International Sanatana Dharma Society (ISDS) fundamentally distinctive when compared to any other Hindu / Dharma / Yoga movement on earth today.

1) **Guru Principle**: We recognize that it is only under the expert guidance and grace of an authentic *guru* that we can traverse the path to liberation safely and effectively. We are guided, both as individual disciples and as a movement, by a living and extremely qualified representative of the Vedic ideal in the form of our enlightened spiritual teacher Sri Acharyaji.

2) **Scripturally-Based**: We scrupulously base everything the ISDS does and teaches upon a clear understanding of the Ve-

dic scriptures. Our approach to philosophy, spiritual practice, meditation and lifestyle are all rooted directly in the teachings of the scriptures. Indeed, in-depth and guided study of the Vedic scriptures is one of the most important ongoing practices that our members engage in.

3) **Academic Excellence**: Our members strongly strive to couple their meditative spiritual practice with a very scholarly and philosophical grasp of the philosophy, theology, culture, history and application of Sanatana Dharma. Mystical attainment can never be used as an excuse for intellectual lethargy on the part of the spiritual practitioner. Success on the spiritual path is only possible with the integrative partnership of both subjective spiritual experience (*anubhava*) coupled with wisdom and understanding (*buddhi*).

4) **Quality over Quantity**: In our philosophy and practices (both personal and as in organizational structure), the ISDS always emphasize the spiritual quality of our activities over mere quantity. Thus, rather than artificially focusing on merely having a large mass following, we instead strive to have a smaller membership of truly exceptional and sincere spiritual practitioners. Consequently, we have sometimes been called somewhat elitist or exclusive in whom we accept as members and formal students. We're fine with that! Our goal is to serve those who are sincerely ready for the real thing: an authentic path the goal of which is having a direct experience of truth. We also seek to create the Dharma leaders and teachers of the future who will carry on the traditions of the most ancient spiritual path on Earth. The ISDS represents nothing less than the cutting-edge Vedic vanguard. The ISDS is thus not for everyone. But if you are willing to learn and practice authentic Vedic spirituality in a mood of humility and sincerity, and to experience growth in your spiritual life in a manner that is truly meaningful, then you are very welcome to join.

5) **Vedic Authenticity**: We are radical traditionalists in our approach to the Vedic way. We seek to practice Dharma in as traditional, authentic, orthodox and uncompromisingly real a manner as is possible in the modern era. There is nothing new, "New Age", or concocted in how we teach or practice the Vedic way. Moreover, we do not "mix and blend" our practice or understanding of Sanatana Dharma with those of other, non-Vedic paths. If you are interested in the ISDS, the teachings of Sri Acharyaji, or being involved in our movement, please do so knowing that what you will be taught and will be following is nothing less than the authentic and ancient religion of Sanatana Dharma - the Eternal Natural Way.

6) **Comprehensiveness**: As students of the Vedic way, we understand that Sanatana Dharma is so much more than merely a religious tradition. Rather, the world-view, arts and sciences of Vedic culture are meant to very naturally extend into every field of human concern. This includes not only the spiritual, but also the social, political, economic, scientific, medical, artistic, musical, culinary, martial, cultural, civilizational and philosophical realms of human endeavor. The ISDS seeks to not only help our members in their own individual spiritual progress, but to also extend the truths of Dharma over the entire sphere of human endeavor. Our goal is to change all of society on the most fundamental of levels, and to thus affect the respiritualization of global civilization.

7) **Effective Sadhana**: The powerful spiritual disciplines that the ISDS teaches its members are highly effective, authorized and scripturally-based, with an emphasis on Yoga, *mantra*, *puja*, and meditation as revealed in the *Upanishads*. Our *sadhana* techniques are known to provide practitioners with an immediate experience of spiritual bliss and realization. At the same time, however, it is understood that sadhana is a long-term commitment that will eventually deepen a person's spiritual realization over time. *Sadhana* is not merely some magical

amusement. It is a commitment.

8) **Highest Ethical Standards**: Many in the West have all too often found themselves exploited by unethical "spiritual teachers" who falsely claimed to be representing the pure Yoga and Dharma tradition, but who only turned out to be amoral abusers of their innocent followers. The ISDS is unyielding in its commitment to upholding and educating all its members in the very highest ethical standards that form the core behavioral expectations of Vedic culture. Our strict code of ethics includes adherence to the Yamas and Niyamas of Yoga philosophy. Both the initiated students and the leaders of the ISDS are expected, without exception, to strictly observe the following ethical standards: a) no intoxicants (including alcohol, cigarettes, marijuana, hashish, ayahuasca, etc.), b) strict lacto-vegetarianism (no meat, fish or eggs), c) no illicit or exploitative sexual behavior (sexuality should be confined exclusively to the institution of marriage). It is only in demanding the very highest ethical standards of its leaders that the dignity of Sanatana Dharma can be upheld.

Becoming a Member of the ISDS

We recognize that membership in the ISDS is not for everyone. Our students are dedicated to following a path that encourages them to look honestly within in a contemplative manner, to observing a spiritual discipline that leads to a gradual unfoldment of their true selves, and that results in Self-realization and God-consciousness.

If you are interested in joining the International Sanatana Dharma Society, we ask that you possess deep sincerity, humility, openness, and a strong desire to know the Divine. If you are attracted to a Vedic-based path that focuses on thorough authenticity, a conscientious philosophical approach, and a clear and effective means of knowing God's presence in your everyday life, please consider becoming an official member today.

The following are requirements for membership:

1. You must consider Sanatana Dharma to be your spiritual tradition.

2. All members are expected to donate monthly in accordance with their means.

Please choose a generous amount below, and start giving your tax-deductible monthly membership donation today!

Membership Tiers

1. **Basic Membership**: $120 minimum annual donation. ($10 per month)
2. **Family Membership**: $240 minimum annual donation. ($20 per month)
3. **Supporting Member (Dharma Warrior)**: $600 minimum annual donation. ($50 per month)
4. **Patron Member (Dharma Knight)**: $1200 minimum annual donation. ($100 per month)
5. **Life Member (Dharma King/Queen)**: $5000 minimum one time donation.

For more information on how to become a member, please visit:

www.dharmacentral.com/membership.html

www.ingramcontent.com/pod-product-compliance
Lightning Source LLC
Chambersburg PA
CBHW051953090426
42741CB00008B/1374

* 9 7 8 0 9 8 6 2 5 2 6 2 4 *